they are of ireland

by Declan Lynch

HOT
PRESS

books

First published in 1994 by Hot Press Books,
13 Trinity Street, Dublin 2

British Library Cataloguing in Publication
Data is available for this book.

ISBN: 0-9524947-0-1

Photographs by Colm Henry, Cathal Dawson and Michael Quinn

Design by Paula Nolan, Hot Press
Cover Design by Michael Crotty
Printed by Future Print

N T R O D U C T I O N

YES, they're all here. And the ones that aren't here will be along any minute now.

With the approach of the Millennium, the development of the "Peace Process", and another Eurovision in the bag, I felt that the time had come to compile some sort of tribute to the extraordinary characters whose words and deeds have contributed so much to the rich tapestry that is "Ireland." Who's who and who's nobody on the national stage.

And why, oh why, oh why?

Hopefully, the work you are now holding in your hands will become a valuable reference book for scholars at home and abroad, though it differs in style from conventional works of reference in being suffused with mockery.

I am indebted to my friends and colleagues who have perused the manuscript and made complimentary remarks in order to humour me. They must share some of the blame. Niall Stokes, Chairman of the IRTC, is particularly culpable in this regard.

I would like to thank the staff of the National Library for their unfailing courtesy and erudition. I haven't been there for 14 years, but I'd like to thank them anyway. They are of Ireland. Come dance with them in Ireland.

I would like also to thank the students at Harvard University, for no good reason I can think of and to everyone at the Tyrone Guthrie Centre, which is supposed to be a great place altogether.

I owe a particular debt to Stephen O'Byrnes of

the Progressive Democrats, whose Euro election poster, "Simply The Best", set this whole unstoppable ride of events in motion. Something inside of me snapped, m'lud.

Many thanks to Paula for laying it out so darn pretty, and to Duan, who knows how to operate my compooter.

Caroline, Adam and our dog Mac were always on hand to offer useful tips and destructive criticism, and my wonderful 6 year-old daughter Roseanne is hoping that this book does well so that she can give up one of her cleaning jobs, and take that trip to Lourdes, please God. It will mean that my operation will have to wait, but you don't want to hear about that.

DECLAN LYNCH
IRELAND 1994

ADAMS, Gerry

Widely criticised as an apologist for the IRA, and hailed as the joint author of the non-existent Hume-Adams Document, Gerry purports to be something of a Renaissance Man, being an author of folksy short stories about gas characters in Belfast. He is also officially "a barman" and was no doubt concerned at the effect of the IRA's bombing campaign on the licencing trade in general. "Shadow Of A Barman" is an obvious biography title. He is unusual for a guerilla spokesperson in looking like a woodwork teacher, and sounded better when his monotonous voice was replaced by that of an actor, due to broadcasting restrictions. Without the benefit of ventriloquism, he still appeals to the media who reckon that he knows people who know where the bodies are buried. Americans loved him for his hilarious performance on the *Larry*

7

King Show. Gay Byrne didn't for his masterful appearance on the *Late Late.* Due to the pristine condition of his hair, you could say that he has dyed for Ireland.

AHERN, Bertie

A veteran American journalist who followed Bertie around on the campaign trail said that he had never seen the like, and he had seen some. The Ahern machine is well-oiled, and is sorry you were out when it called, even when you were in. He is never Ahern, always "Bertie", and we feel warmly protective towards him when he talks about "grote" in the economy, or mentions his dealings with the Bundesbank. The Finance portfolio has forced him to stop wearing anoraks and forswear making throwaway remarks in interviews about drinking a gallon of Bass and driving home. We can empathise with "Bertie", but we are still coming to terms with Mr. Ahern. He hasn't quite got the hang of it himself.

ALDRIDGE, John

We grew to love "Aldo" for his persistent failure to score a goal for Ireland, despite being the darling of Oxford, Liverpool, Real Sociedad and Tranmere, where he scored goals with almost nauseating frequency. Eventually he began to hit the onion sack for the Republic, but only against countries like Tunisia, Malta, Latvia and Albania, who had it coming to them. When he "scored" against Spain in Seville, the goal was disallowed, not for offside, as was alleged, but simply because it was Aldo. His grandmother is from Athlone, and not a lot of

people know that a man called John Aldridge was once the choirmaster and organist at St. Mary's Church in Athlone. They are entirely unrelated, except through their country of birth, which is England.

ALLEN, Darina

During the '80's, the TV chef became a celebrity, and Ireland responded with Darina of Ballymaloe House. While her English rivals tended to be borderline madmen, Darina wielded a sensible skillet, faddish only in her choice of spectacles. For the primitive cook, her declared aim of using accessible ingredients raised a few eyebrows with the inclusion in *Simply Delicious 2* of things such as walnut oil, raddichio trevisano, and lardons. Lardons? Like her butter, that one needs clarification.

ALLEN, Foster And

Borne on the wings of one-time manager Donie Cassidy's vaulting ambitions, the duo startled an entire nation by appearing on *Top Of The Pops* in kilts, explaining that they were a part of the then popular New Romantic movement. Like much of the Cassidy stable, they played at half-time in the All-Ireland Final, soothing the nerves of the spectators with those languid tunes which are best appreciated after a tube of Mogodon. Though they have sold albums on a U2 scale, only the aficionadoes are able to tell which one is Foster and

which is Allen. They don't seem to mind.
See Cassidy, Donie.

AMSBY, Alan
See Pussy, Mister.

ANDREWS, David
Easier on the eye than brother Niall, he revelled in Foreign Affairs, being praised in the *International Herald Tribune* for his Somalia initiative. The restless spirits of "Albert" and "Dick" quickly put a halt to that gallop, and subsequently he languished in the Marine, not the foreign affair he would have chosen. He represents Dun Laoghaire, where they like their Fianna Failers to have fully evolved.

ANDREWS, Niall
A "Charlie Man" to the tip of his beak, he is most famously photographed in the midst of a crowd of wild-eyed zealots, fearing that the end of Charlie is nigh, and in vigilant mode. He loves the camera but the camera does not always reciprocate. He is a lively companion and a committed European, who brings much *joie de vivre* to the perfumed halls of Brussels.

ARKLE
The great steeplechaser transcended the mere equine to become the Spirit of the Nation, trouncing the English champion Mill House as we stood and roared at our television sets, proclaiming revenge for Skibbereen long

before anyone had ever heard of Ray Houghton. "This is the champion, this is the best we've seen for a long time," said Peter O'Sullivan, as Arkle charged up the hill at Cheltenham to claim another Gold Cup. Though Arkle is no longer with us in the flesh, I include him here in a special category, that of the legendary individual who happened to be a horse.

ASMAL, Kader

One of our own in all but nationality, the founder of the Irish Anti-Apartheid movement is a now a big noise in the new South Africa, where his knowledge of Irish electoral mores will alert him to the possibility of Chief Buthelezi's supporters voting early and often. We see him having the craic with Mandela, and say, "there's Kader, one of our own." He may never get used to the idea of fascists having to be nice to him, but at least he can eat all the oranges he likes.

ATTLEY, Bill

The former League of Ireland referee is now in charge of SIPTU, issuing yellow cards to those who display the unacceptable face of capitalism. Union leaders, of course, tend to be "barons", suggesting that they are descended from one of Europe's noble families which has fallen on hard times. Genealogists have so far failed to trace Bill back to the Hozenzollerns, or the Rainiers, or the Romanovs but commentators still stick to the "baron" tag. The Red Baron, perhaps?
See Ross, Shane.

BALLAGH, Robert

In an extraordinary marriage between art and commerce, the richer you are, the more of his work you possess. You can either collect his paintings, or accumulate vast quantities of banknotes designed by him. While creating art that the ordinary man can carry around in his jeans, and back horses with, "Bobby" also attracts controversy on the artistic wing of the Republican movement. His "Time For Peace - Time To Go" movement, conspicuously lacked a question mark at the end.

BANIM, Al

He is our only working stand-up comedian whose name sounds like that of a Middle Eastern terrorist. Al Ban-eem, a sort of rival to Abu Nidal. Will he tell a mother-in-law joke or hold the audience capture? On a good night, he will do both.

BANVILLE, John

"I don't pretend to be a dramatist. I did this because I want to get Kleist onto the Dublin stage." No-one else could have said this, because very few people apart from John Banville have heard of Kleist, let alone gone out on a limb to bring him to the Dublin stage. Banville is thought to be a genius, who writes beautiful novels about scientists, mathematicians, and associated interesting headcases. He is not widely loved, because he is more in the "European" tradition, avoiding popular Irish themes of a young man coming to terms with his sexuality in the '50's, the problems of priestcraft, or peasants on the verge of a nervous breakdown. The fastidious word-conjurer once spoke in an interview of "a rage for order", reminding you that he used to be a sub-editor in the *Irish Press,* where there is characteristically " a rage for last orders."
See MacArthur, Malcolm.

BARRY, Joe

Director-General of RTE, he is best known for being pictured at the Eurovision Song Contest each year, wondering whether to laugh or cry. While his predecessor boasted the initials "T.V.", Joe has no such natural advantages.

13

The general public seems largely unaware of his views on anything other than the Eurovision.

BARRY, Oliver

Eclectic impresario, who saw the potential for bums on seats in artistes as diverse as The Wolfe Tones, James Last and Michael Jackson, as well as orchestrating the odd Fianna Fail Ard-Fheis, where bums on seats is not a problem. When his career as a media mogul came to an end with Century Radio, his long-haired opponents found the idea of Oliver metaphorically flushing money into the ocean to be an amusing one. No doubt he saw the funny side of it too, when the fumes abated.

BARRY, Peter

Perhaps his problem reflected that of Fine Gael in general, the feeling that these people are not hungry enough for power, are not con- torted with lust for the prize, because they are too rich in the first place to abase themselves before us in the required fashion. This would not apply to Gay Mitchell, but it applies in spades to a tea magnate like Peter Barry, a fine and cultivated *gintleman* who didn't seem to need the approval of the scurvy mob. Why would people like this want to run the country when they could be out enjoying themselves?

BARRY-MURPHY, Jimmy

The only skinhead to star in an All-Ireland Final. The diehards didn't know where to gawk as he won the match for Cork while looking distinctly marginalised from society. The tides of fashion, and the need to make a living, ultimately persuaded him to style his hair like other men, but there are still those who look back on those shaven images, searching the screen for a Stanley knife. The thicks. A wizard, a true star.

BASKIN, Bibi

Reluctant sweetheart of the rodeo, the darling of middle Ireland, she cultivated the grassroots in both national languages. Her television career to date has been like an endless tour of the rubber chicken circuit, a dark and lonely job which someone has to do. Each interview with a raddled showband relic made you wonder whether she has to drink with them as well, or if it was strictly business. On a radio phone-in, a caller declared that he would like to be buried, not on land or sea, but "up to my balls in Bibi Baskin." She will not pine for such things, now that she plies her trade beyond the foam.

BEGLEY, Philomena

She is the Queen of Country to Ray Lynam's King. Together, they emulate the duets of Tammy Wynette and George "No Show" Jones without the maniacal drinking and drug-taking and bad craziness. So it's easier for them, but still admirable. Phil taught Daniel O'Donnell everything that he knows, but obviously not everything that she knows.

See Furey, Finbarr; Lynam, Ray; O'Donnell, Daniel.

BENNIS, Nora

Leader of Solidarity, another splinter of the Anti-Happiness League which abhors the "liberal agenda", she went

to Brighton once to see Mother Teresa, but Mother never showed. Aw, shucks. So she came back to campaign for the Irish Catholic Family, rent asunder by the filthy modern tide. Solidarity now has a political wing. Is there a military alternative? For Nora, the violets are not scenting the woods.

BINCHY, Maeve

An incredibly pleasant woman, she dispels the myth that writers are supposed to be gaunt and haggard. They soon start to bloom when they shift units in Binchy proportions. At one stage, she appeared set to write a book of short stories about every station in the London Underground, but later shifted her gaze to the *Lilac Bus,* as her muse took root in the Ireland of her memory. "Her books are as hard to pick up as they are to put down."

BINCHY, William

Law Professor at Trinity College and zealous protector of the unborn, he is a brother to Maeve, who can't understand where Willy got it from. Perhaps he picked it up on a foreign holiday. He provides an intellectual dimension to the fever of the pro-Life movement, who can say, "we have this on the authority of an eminent professor." Still, he was, to say the least, alarmed when his beloved Pro-Life amendment was later interpreted by the Supreme Court as permitting abortion in certain circumstances. He decided that they were wrong, and that we now had the most liberal abortion laws in Europe, though, in fact, we have no abortion here at all, since we get our abortions in England. How does he get his head around it all? An opponent remarked, "I'll say this for Willy, he's got balls." And in a manner of speaking he probably had a point.

See Hanafin, Des ; Lucey, Dr. Mary ; Bennis, Nora.

BIRD, Charlie

The Birdman of Montrose once preached revolution, but is now the nation's favourite doorstepper. They chant his name in public as he camps outside the Dail to get the verdict on a Fianna Fail heave. From Iraq to The Phillipines, his voice has been heard, loud and clear — but especially loud. He once spent a week's wages on flowers for his intended, which was both very romantic and a hell of a good story. In love as in journalism, his persistence paid off.

BOLGER, Dermot

Barbara Cartland is prolific, but Bolger is trotting after, not least because his quantity is suffused with quality, and he doesn't have the advantage of a stately home, a fleet of secretaries, and readers who spend most of the day wondering where their shoes are. His labours done, he sets about publishing the works of other writers, building a paper mountain where once there was nothing. Then he has a round of golf. Mmm, the Irish golfing novel needs a bit of a boost.

BONNER, Packie

It was hard to indulge in Packie-bashing even after he opened the floodgates to Holland in America '94. He kept England out in Stuttgart, he ruined the lives of countless Rumanians in Genoa, and he was practically our playmaker under the Charlton banner. Go gentle into that good night.

BOOTHMAN, Jack

He was the first large Protestant to become President of the GAA, which is justifiably proud of this lurch towards pluralism. Withal, he is sound enough on the national question.

Besides, he doesn't really look like a Protestant.

BOWMAN, John

A journalist who works in broadcasting. He found it necessary to clarify this job-description when a caller to his radio show characterised him as "a disc-jockey". He continued to sport psychedelic ties even after this shocking incident, consoling himself with fine wines. He has maintained an eerie silence on the career of his son, the famous Jonathan Philbin, perhaps jealous of the latter's superior wardrobe. Sayings include, "the gentleman at the back with his hand up", and "you've been in already."

BRADY, Liam

The arrival of Big Jack signalled the international demise of "Chippy", revered from the butt end of Belmullet to the heel of Italy and even the Horn of Africa for what Jack regarded as "fannying around". That left foot was so educated, he must have got it from the Sorbonne. "He is financially secure."

BRENNAN, Seamus

Little Seamus first came to mass attention on RTE Election Specials, where he emerged as an expert on voting patterns throughout the ages. The ace psephologist was once described as "the least repulsive face of Fianna Fail" at a time when the Party's affairs seemed to be directed by Roman Polanski. He can be trusted with money.
See Doherty, Sean.

BROWNE, Noel

Rather than waste his life kissing episcopal ass, he set about eradicating T.B. The people loved him for this, but the hierarchy felt that he might be better employed perpetuating the oppression of women. His mega-selling autobiography, *Against The Tide,* recalled a life in politics in which, after many tribulations, the author is invariably proved correct by end of chapter.

BROWNE, Vincent

As head honcho at the *Sunday Tribune* he was probably the only newspaper editor in the world with a distrust of "good writing", which he regarded as a form of cheating. Words like "mercurial", "unpredictable", "brilliant", and "sexy", can only offer a scant flavour of this man. Like the fabled offspring of Daniel O'Connell, there was a time when you couldn't throw a stone into a Baggot Street pub without hitting a former editor of *Magill.* His dismissal from the editor's chair at the *Turbine* has not curbed his forensic passion, which he has brought to the fields of philosophy and law, and to newspaper columns which leave the readers tired but happy.

BRUTON, John

"Decent", "hard-working", "sincere", and "VAT on children's shoes" are the buzz-words here, characteristics which were unattractive to elements within Fine Gael, who sought his removal from the role of leader when the Party hit new depths in the polls. His persona is a bit on the bucolic side to attract floating voters, who find decency, industry, and sincerity to be excellent qualities in one's plumber, but not necessarily in a leader of the free world, especially when he barks like a seal. Clongowes-educated, owner of a ranch, he has much to be sincere about, while slippier customers get on with running the country into the ground.

BUCKLEY, Fr. Pat

"They called it Wanker's Corner." Thus began a *Hot Press* article about the rebel priest, in which he described how seminarians at Clonliffe would be exposed to civilian ridicule when they arrived in chapel of a morning to confess their nocturnal emissions. He performs wedding ceremonies for couples on their second stab at matrimony, and has alienated the affections of his superiors, criticising the lofty opinion of Cardinal Daly on the perfume of his own farts. Darling of the media, who are sure that he will let more and bigger cats out of the bag, he is Ireland's most eligible priest.
See Casey, Bishop.

BURGH, Chris De

"There's a Spanish Train that runs from Guadalquivir to old Seville." Though slated by the critics for his chocolate-box romanticism and his gormless statements of the eternal verities, Chris is the crown prince of single-bar electric fire land, and became a global phenomenon when he sang about a lady in red, *dawncing* with him. His fame increased after his

porksword came into contact with the help. After an IRA atrocity, he sang a song on the *Late Late Show* which declared that he was ashamed to be Irish. Born in Argentina, the holder of a British passport, he probably has less to be ashamed about than most. He is unhappy with the taxation system. And sometimes he is just unhappy.

BURKE-KENNEDY, Mary Elizabeth

A quare name but great stuff.
See Frisbee, Mai and Stewart-Liberty, Nell.

BYRNE, Gabriel

You can tell that he has a social conscience. As his name becomes more glamorous, his film roles become increasingly sordid, a desperate collection of smack barons, alcoholic gangsters, alcoholic travellers, and other such Irish perennials. He was once thinking of becoming a priest, the one really challenging Irish role that he turned down. Good call, Gabriel.

BYRNE, Gay

"The greatest broadcaster in the world, bar none." No-one can claim to be a serious player until they have been anointed on the *Late Late Show*. His sayings include "one for everyone in the audience", "excirra and delirra", "the country is banjaxed" and "our friends on Channel 4." He has a strong sexual attraction to Jane Fonda, and is himself the object of fantastic yearnings on the part of women, to whom he is a counsellor, a friend, a surrogate husband who talks to them in a friendly manner without expecting them to cook his dinner or wash his clothes. Gaybo hates the IRA, pseudo-intellectuals, and flamboyant accountants. He loves jazz, Peter Ustinov and Mother Teresa of Calcutta. No-one can decide whether he is fabulously rich or dirt poor, a confusion which he seems to share.

CAMPBELL-SHARPE, Noelle

A driven woman, she has applied her energies to publishing, aerobics, our national heritage and lately rock'n'roll management, with a single-mindedness reminiscent of her hero, Napoleon. She encourages "drive" in others, and likes the kind of interviewees who say that they are ultimately after her job. So if you are interviewed for a post in, say, Bord Na Mona, and they ask you where you want to be in five years time, tell them that you want Noelle Campbell-Sharpe's job, and it should be oxo.

CARNEY, Judge Paul

He fell into controversy due to a disturbance outside the Shelbourne Hotel. It was surely some kind of turning point in history when a judge couldn't get a drink after hours. We have all been that judge.

CARROLL, John

The former head of the ITGWU became even more interesting when it was revealed in a biography of Petra Kelly that he had had a "close connection" with the Green heroine. And why not? He had a lovely, panoramic view of Dublin from his office.

CASEY, Bishop

In New York they were calling him "the 200-pound Irish bishop with woman and money problems," as he fled his diocese for a spot of "re-education", leaving a trail of emotional and financial havoc. His American lover Annie Murphy told fabulous tales of romance on Inch Strand, of floating on gossamer wings, of kinky sex practices, and the consumption of expensive brandy with the high-rolling, fast-living, sheepdog-battering Casey. The fruit of their passion was Peter, now an American teenager who shopped his dear old dad for his reluctance to bond. With his pectoral cross flapping in the wind, there was a despairing damage-limitation exercise, as streams of callers rang up RTE to talk about their father, the priest. The ebullient Casey now resides in Ecuador, where he runs a mission and grants the occasional interview, embarrassing the hierarchy with his forays to the World Cup and to visit old friends in a variety of disguises. Sayings include, "do ye all know who I am?" and "take it off, Annie." *Annie get your gun!*

CASSIDY, Donie

Showband mogul, musician, songwriter, hotelier, proprietor of Wax Museum and Senator, Donie gets a bang for his buck in a bewildering variety of ways. The phrase "he knows all the angles" assumes alarming proportions here, as the camera invariably picks him out close to the vortex of the action. He is ubiquitous in the manner of Woody Allen's "Zelig". "Senator" is a useful title when he goes to Nashville, where

24

a Senator actually means something, and a "TD" evokes images of venereal disease. He wrote 'Arise And Follow Charlie' and added gunshots to the end of the T.R. Dallas epic 'Who Shot J.R. Ewing', proving his acute understanding of the authentic desires of the hidden Ireland. "I don't drink, I don't smoke, and I have excess time," he said. In 1963, he lost 3 people who were very important to him: John F. Kennedy, Pope John XXIII and Jim Reeves.

CHAMPIONS, Gina, Dale Haze And The

What was all that about?

CHARLTON, Jack

Midway through his tenure, commentators stopped calling him a typical gruff Yorkshireman and called him a typical gruff Geordie, which was more accurate. Eventually they called him an Irishman, though not a typical one. Jack called people all sorts of things, but usually not their given name. He

called Paul McGrath "John", and much besides. He called Bulgaria "Rumania", he called Albania "Rumania", as well. He called it as he saw it, even if it wasn't that at all. But he knew what he wanted to see, and when the game was played to his liking: when the light caught them in a certain way his favourite team of all time was Northampton Town.

CHEVRON, Philip

It is not widely known that *Ghostown,* by The Radiators, is the best Irish record ever made. The boy Chevron made most of it. Pioneer of punk, pioneer of the Brechtian influence in Irish pop (oh yes!) and pioneer of pop based on *Ulysses* (oh yes!), he joined The Pogues, and was the first pioneer they had ever met. He is one of the Chevrons of Santry.

CLARE, Dr. Anthony

The thinking man's Terry Wogan, he discovered a new branch of medicine, Celebrity Psychiatry. He persuaded people to tell him their most embarrassing secrets, though they weren't even trying to flog a book or a movie. On his triumphant return to Erin, there was some talk about him entering politics. It was hard to visualise him sitting cheek by jowl with Brian Cowen at an Ard-Fheis. He wisely demurred. The psychiatrist must not himself become mad.

CLAYTON, Adam

In the era of clean-living pop icons, Adam has re-dressed the balance somewhat in favour of the rock'n'roll verities by appearing on drugs charges, behaving in an unorthodox manner in hotel rooms, and hanging out with pouting babes. The core values burn bright in the Clayton soul. He is thought to be the luckiest man alive.

COLGAN, Michael

With artistic and commercial acumen, he has provided Dubliners with many wonderful and tasteful evenings at The Gate, of which everyone says, "it's very small, but lovely. Very small, you know." He is almost unique in theatrical circles in being constantly sober. This must be very difficult where plays are concerned, but I suppose there's nothing in his contract which says he has to watch them.

COLLINS, Gerard

He let it be known that as Foreign Minister, he preferred to be called "Gerard". Others had already rechristened him "Luigi", due to his Italianate features, and his high standing in the Cosa Nostra that is Fianna Fail. While he was at it, he volunteered a new name for the South African President, Mr. "De Clark". He loved Foreign Affairs, but the public loved him most for his lachrymose appeal on television to Albert Reynolds not to burst up the Party. Reynolds didn't exactly burst up the Party, but he let the air out of Gerard somewhat.

COLLINS, Ronan

It is not widely known that the popular afternoon disc-jockey does very fine impersonations of colleagues such as Micheál O'Muircheartaigh. When impersonating himself, he supervises the shenanigans on RTE's *Play The Game*, which is difficult, as he is always sober. In idle moments, one wonders how much he gets paid for hosting the Lotto. He shaved his moustache off when Michael Carruth won the gold medal.

COMERFORD, Chris

Much maligned victim of the Greencore Scandal, like the navvies of old, he worked all day for the sugar in his tay. And he worked nights too. Around the time of his sad departure from the sweet life, there was much malign media discussion of a Golden Circle of rich persons becoming alarmingly richer by unsavoury means, and of unacceptable levels of greed. This seems to have stopped now, so everything is all right again, thank God.

COMISKEY, Bishop

From his palace in Ferns, he keeps a censorious eye on media matters, suspecting for some strange reason that the heathens of Dublin 4 are less interested in reflecting the views of Catholics than they are in writing profiles of priests' love-children. In his *Irish Catholic* column, he accused the present writer of blasphemy, an annoying charge when one was not even trying to be blasphemous at the time, and felt hung for a lamb as distinct from a sheep. His "with-it" hairstyle presents an agreeable image to the media-saturated world, and he is generally considered to be the pin-up boy of the Irish hierarchy.

See Casey, Bishop.

CONNELL, Archbishop

"He may know a lot about angels, but he knows nothing about fairies." Critics perceive a lack of human warmth in him, as he expounds the old orthodoxies. Supporters perceive this too. In the era of Big Ed Casey, the Church has had enough of human warmth.

See Casey, Bishop.

COSTELLO, Yvonne

The Miss Ireland crown acted as a springboard to a varied career, including a role in Lee

Dunne's *Goodbye To The Hill,* and a shop which sold unusual underwear, suits made of rubber, and many fine things which the Irish were not accustomed to. So beautiful, so talented.

See Treacy, Olivia.

COUGHLAN, Mary

"Just like Francis of Assisi, you're so kind to the animal in me." For such glorious couplets, Galway's blues queen is a mighty presence in our culture. In the war against obscurantism and dread, she has sung a soldier's song.

COULTER, Phil

It is impossible to consume a meal in an Irish restaurant any more without the saccharine sounds of Coulter seeping through the walls of your stomach. Aficionadoes prefer his work with the Bay City Rollers, when people used to scream rather than peruse the set menu. He should specify which of his albums go with fish and which are ideal for vegetarians. For the beef, you need Ted Nugent.

COWEN, Brian

"If in doubt, leave them out," he roared from an Ard-Fheis platform, goading the hated PD's and finding the collective G-spot of the Fianna Fail Party. He became the Party's chief warm-up man in succession to Brian Lenihan, a context in which he can be regarded as "bright" and "young" and "a bull." He is not feeling quite so bullish however since he was found to have shares in Arcon — a mining company licenced by his own Department. He denies having had anything to do with deleting a certain sentence. Thousands would believe him.

COX, Pat

Taking the PD gospel to its ultimate apotheosis, Pat Cox privatised himself, laying low the Desocrats on the altar of his own vaulting ambitions. Mr. O'Malley will not be seeking out the company of Pat "Mad Dog" Cox on the Provisional wing of the Party. But there is a downside to this as well. It can not be easy for a man to maintain such a healthy ego without endangering some other vital organ along the way. Look what happened to poor John Bobbitt.

CRIBBEN, Mena

A firebrand of Tridentine re-armament, she considers the present Pope to be a liberal, preferring a more sulphurous kind of Catholicism in which there are no guitars. Her unbending views on sexual morality, in which single mothers are "mistresses", reside with no apparent contradiction alongside a strain of militant republicanism. She was given a holiday in New York by the *Late Late Show* for volunteering to be the target for a professional knife-thrower. He was accurate, but not deadly.

CUDDY, Joe

He expressed regret that Jason Donovan's version of 'Any Dream Will Do' became a massive international hit some twenty years after the Cuddy version. Well, Jason is a boyish Australian sex symbol and megastar, while Joe is a middle-aged Irish cabaret singer with a name that rhymes with "cruddy". These are the breaks.

CUNNINGHAM, Larry

His life has been one of almost uninterrupted success as a National Teacher, a proprietor of a mini-market and dry-cleaners, a Mercedes driver, and a crooner of sentimental ballads. With his distinctive accordion-pleated hairstyle and neat dress, he was something of a heart-throb for lonely Midland women, who sighed at his evocations of Lovely Leitrim, Slaney Valley, and various towns in Tipperary. He lives in Granard.

CURRIE, Austin

Comic writings in *Hot Press* had Austin still expecting to win the Presidency, because the feedback he was getting on the doorsteps bore no relation to the opinion polls. When informed that Mrs. Robinson had in fact been President for the past 18 months, he dismissed it as "media hype". Austin was not put out by this. He has been through worse.

DALY, Cardinal

In common with Dr. Ian Paisley, he shares the vocal mannerism of whistling the letter "s", which can be something of a distraction when one's vocabulary is rich in references to sectarianism, sadness, sympathy, sincerity, and the sin of sodomy. He has a feminine quality which is attractive to some elderly people, and he seemed beatifically happy when he was made a Cardinal. As you would be. A frequent critic of the Provisional IRA, he sees no future in integrated schooling as a step across the great divide. At Christmas, he gets together with Dr. Robin Eames of the Church of Ireland.

32

They laugh and joke and pray for peace. A temperate man, he still enjoys a good pilgrimage whenever he gets the opportunity. He did not report the paedophile priest Fr. Brendan Smyth to the police.

See Casey, Bishop; Smyth, Fr. Brendan.

DANAHER, Gerry

One of our most famous barristers, he became involved in some quare unpleasantness when the Bar Council investigated remarks made in the Shelbourne Hotel. His old friend Adrian Hardiman acknowledged that the remarks were made "in drink", while reserving a certain moral fury that anything associated with the Beef Tribunal might be viewed as improper. Though abnormally wealthy, the former Sinn Fein activist and putative Attorney General is said to make quiet donations to charity.

See Hardiman, Adrian.

DANIELS, Roly

They say that he had the most luscious lips on the entire showband scene. Where is he now, and where are his lips?

D'ARCY, Fr. Brian

"He loves to laugh." Confessor to the Irish showbusiness industry, he has much to laugh about. Oh, the things that he has heard, the sins he has forgiven. As part of his "with-it" vocation, he laughs at a lot of things which are not necessarily funny at all. But then, if you weren't laughing, you'd be crying, as he might say in his jolly *Sunday World* column, "A Little Bit Of Religion". The question is, can you be a little bit religious, or is it like being a little bit pregnant? Still, he loves to laugh.

See Casey, Bishop.

DAVIS, Derek

The cosmopolitan Northerner was renowned for being fat. Then he was renowned for not being nearly as fat as he had been. For the versatile Derek, size is important. Part of him is Protestant, another part is Catholic, and a third part just wants to have a good time, and get paid a lot. Variety is in his blood.

DAY-LEWIS, Daniel

Dan The Man has declared for Ireland, and would be eligible to play for the Republic if he so chose. Then again, Sean McBride was eligible to play for France and The Republic, and never answered the call. Given the majestic sweep of his virtuosity, he could conceivably act the centre-half role a lot better than Alan Kernaghan. It seems that every woman in Christendom wants to shag him, just the once. He will do himself an injury some day.

DELANEY, Frank

The drinking man's Anthony Clare, the thinking woman's crumpet, RTE could only imagine him as a newsreader. They failed to see that he was a bibliophile, an elegant writer and broadcaster, and not at all posh. The BBC took one look at him and said, "where have you been all our lives?". In Tipperary, mostly, brushing up his act. There was no crumpet in Tipperary, as such.

DESMOND, Dermot

Dubbed "The Kaiser" by Michael Smurfit, a typically witty reference to his distinctive moustache and imperious mastery of the financial services sector, he became something of a German spectacle in the furore over the sale of the Telecom site in Ballsbridge. As with the less-than-excellent performance of the NCB Ireland round-the-world yacht, few wept openly in the streets as the pressure mounted on the moustachioed entrepreneur. These are problems we could all handle in our own way. He has lived in Afghanistan. Perhaps he might go back there. He may or may not be a friend of Charles J. Haughey.

DEVLIN, Alan

The gifted thespian has brought new levels of improvisation to the Irish stage, most notably during a performance of *HMS Pinafore*, when he departed the stage in mid-oration to continue the performance at a nearby bar. Perhaps the most exciting figure in contemporary Irish theatre, you can never predict his next move, and up to a point, neither can he.

35

DICEMAN, The

Dublin's renowned street characters such as Bang Bang and Johnny Fortycoats have long been eclipsed by Tom McGinty, The Diceman. Here was a moving statue without tears, a street performer to whom you would give money to stay, rather than to go somewhere. France, for example.

DOCTORS, The Saw

Thanks to the economic vandalism wrought by the monetarist ethic, the Saw Doctors became spokespeople for a lost generation, when they might well have passed their days shovelling sugar at the factory in Tuam. Their concerts attract huge crowds at home and abroad, but because they have so many friends, it is somewhat doubtful that anyone has actually paid in to see them. The accordion-player fecked off after winning the Lotto.

DOHERTY, Sean

There are people on the stuffy end of politics who don't like the cut of his jib, a matter of rich amusement to his followers, who see him as God in a blue serge suit. Superstar of the GUBU era, he will be forever remembered as long as people use the telephone. A noted wit, the former Minister for Justice defended the construction of a high wall around his house on the grounds that it stopped Seamus Brennan looking in at him. He represents a time when running the coun-

try was a barrel of laughs, when Ireland was free of Progressive Democrats, and when the Minister for Justice was expected to be an accomplished ballroom dancer.

DOLAN, Joe

Mullingar's answer to Demis Roussos, he is, amazingly, still hitting the high notes, unlike, say, Freddie Mercury, another falsetto warbler who busted sanctions by playing in South Africa. At least Joe had sponsored a few black babies as a lad, so in showband terms, they owed him. An "ambassador of song", he played the Soviet Union when it was neither profitable nor popular, showing that the West was still the best. Joe sings. Empires crumble.

DOYLE, Mick

"Doyler" caused reverberations of shock among the rugby fraternity by announcing that he likes women. There are alickadoos who still harbour the hope that he will change his mind, and get real. Niall Toibin has a sketch in which a character describes Charles J. Haughey launching the "Doyler" autobiography. The character is unimpressed, because it is "a book about rugby and ridin'. And, sure, Charlie Haughey knows nothing about rugby."

DOYLE, Roddy

The gentle pedagogue turned millionaire author can but smile as the wise heads of the

Department of Education propose to introduce his works to the Leaving Cert syllabus. There is much debate as to whether his gurrier anti-heroes such as Deco Cuffe and Charlo Spencer are suitable material for embryonic minds, or whether it is all me bollix. He is the only winner of the Booker Prize who was cheered by people in pubs. It is hard to imagine A.S. Byatt causing ructions in the Submarine Bar. Doyler has put it on public record that he does not wear pyjamas. Does A. S. Byatt wear pyjamas? Does anyone care?

DREW, Ronnie

One day, in Dublin Zoo, Ronnie Drew was feeling a bit rheumy-eyed as he looked at one of the exotic birds. It was a talking bird, and it said, "hello, Ronnie Drew." He got a terrible fright, swore "never again", and sought out a Zoo operative, who told him that the woman who had donated the bird had trained it to say "hello, Ronnie Drew" to everyone with a beard. Things like that happen, when you are a Dubliner.

DUFFY, Joe

The heir to the Gaybo estate has been learning the business by dealing directly with the public while the old boy sorts out the grand strategies. Whether dealing with prisoners of Mountjoy, or prisoners of the nine-to-five variety, he has the common touch. As Joe Dufflecoat, the radical student leader, he was rarely seen without a megaphone about his person. The radio is a more intimate medium for getting his message across. If he can think of one. Sonny Knowles is his favourite singer.

DUGGAN, Noel C.

The man who put Millstreet on the map. Technically, it was on the map anyway, but people could find few reasons for going there until Noel C. began to dream his impossible dreams. Inspired by the success of his showjumping extravaganzas, he decided that rural Ireland has as much right to the Eurovision as anywhere else, and so it came to pass. Thus, Millstreet is the only place in the world in which both horses and people have been awarded *quatre points* for their troubles. The great facilitator was less than gruntled when BBC newsreader Nicholas Witchell spoke of the Eurovision being held in "a cow-shed". Witchell retracted and rightly so. It was, of course, a horse-shed. Few people know what the "C" stands for, but that doesn't matter. In Ireland, to be known by your initial is part of the honours system.

DUIGNAN, Sean

"Diggy", in the parlance of Protestant head-stones, "went over to the other side." After asking hard questions on the *Six One News,* he became the Government Press Secretary, who sought to forewarn of hard questions on the *Six One News,* or any other News that "Albert" might be troubled by. His many friends in journalism wished him well in his retirement.

DULLY, Martin

Former majordomo of Aer Lingus and Bord Fáilte, in a sparkling interview with Gay Byrne, he reminisced about his childhood in Athlone, where he would sit on the Shannon bridge and admire the passage of traffic to the West. He said that when the light caught it a certain way, you could imagine that you were at the crossroads of the world. Any man growing up in Athlone in the '40s who could see himself at the crossroads of the world was the right man to be running Bord Fáilte.

DUNN, Fr. Joe

A maker of documentary films about religion, he caused some turbulence in ecclesiastical circles with his book, *No Lions In The Hierarchy*, which attacked the present Pope as a rigid conservative who encourages similar rigidity in his bishops. The Pope then broke his leg in the bath.

DUNNE, Ben

He was a regular supermarket baron until he went to Orlando on his holidays, called up a big fat hooker, attempted to snort a rake of Columbian marching powder, and was discovered on the hotel balcony, threatening to fly. A "man's man", he was contrite before the world's media, despite the fact that he had hitherto avoided these pariahs in the style of Ben Senior, whose idea of an interview consisted of repeating the words, "Dunnes Stores better value beats them all." After his eventful vacation, his domination of the family firm began to wane, until his stake was worth a paltry £100 million, or so. His escort meanwhile still lives in a trailer park.

DUNNE, Lee

"The booze, the birds, and the Bob Hope" no longer exercise much fascination for the snowy-haired scribe. Lee has found peace by thinking positively about "life", and by doing the odd half-marathon. He has to his name the monumental Cabbie trilogy, epic tales of promiscuity and taxi-driving. His raunchy *Goodbye To The Hill* ran for ages at the Regency Hotel, suggesting that the future of Irish theatre may depend on the introduction of full bar facilities. A sign in the Men's toilet read, "Gentlemen, if you must speak while you leak, please do it quietly," signed by the author. He has the common touch.

DUNPHY, Eamon

A lot of people knew Eamon Dunphy when he was in short trousers, playing for Ireland during the Dark Ages of moral victories. Perhaps this is why they have followed his career with such intensity, occasionally surrounding his car at the airport to voice their critiques of his journalistic opinions. He has questioned the popular view of Jack Charlton, John Hume and Michel Platini as gods, and the Green Army rose up against him for saying that he was ashamed to be Irish, including those who were aware that he did not say this at all. The Erich Von Stroheim of Irish letters, the man they love to hate, he has explained the difference between good players and great players, between "character" and "decentskinmanship" on innumerable occasions. When he failed to materialise alongside John Giles on the America '94 panel, a nation mourned.

See Giles, John.

DUKES, Alan

As leader of Fine Gael, there were those who thought that he was the problem and John Bruton was the solution, until further reverses seemed to indicate that Bruton was the problem and Dukes the solution. Ridiculed as a person who would be holding a fork when it was raining soup, there are some who will look back on his leadership as virtually a golden age, and others who feel that it wouldn't make much difference if Sonny Knowles was handed the baton. His most effective debating ploy is sarcasm, and he once called a bishop a bastard, which softened his image as a grey number-cruncher. He also flaunted convention by smoking in public. Though not the most charismatic of deputies, he is certainly one of the tallest.

DURCAN, Paul

Our greatest living stand-up poet, he squirts honey in the ears of his listeners with his seductive timbre. He can salute the achievements of both Knock Airport and Sid Vicious without compromising his art. The punters get

a good laugh out of his more accessible lines, and say fair play to him, even though he's got a funny voice. He likes paintings, and writes poems about them. The book *Crazy About Women* was excellent value for money, a prime stocking-filler, and contained many fine poems which were comprehensible to the reader. It is the ultimate tribute to a poet that even stupid people like his stuff. Rave on, Paul Durcan, rave on.

See Morrison, Van.

EDDIE, Electric

The notorious 2FM disc-jockey exercises the intellect in an historical sense, as scholars explore the annals in search of a Saint Electric after whom he might have been named. They find nothing, and instead wonder how a man can go about his daily business in this way. "Good morning, Electric." "Can I rely on your vote, Electric?" Strange.

For God's sake use a condom.

EDGE, The

In U2, he is the deep one. When Bono hollers "this is the Edge," we stand back and gasp at the astonishing layers of noise which emerge from his hands and feet, calling to mind everything from the frenzy of Jimi Hendrix to the sufferings of the people of El Salvador. We see another side to his myriad talents when he whips out the old acoustic and sings 'Van Diemen's Land', a Gaelic lament which turns The Edge into An t-Edge. The satirical group The Joshua Trio have written: *"The Edge has got his hat on/Hip hip hip hooray/The Edge has got his hat on and he's coming out to*

43

play", a reference to the interesting headgear which disguises his baldness. Colleagues call him "Edge", because "The" is too formal. It is an unusual Christian name, one he shares with the 1916 hero, The O'Rahilly.

ENYA

They say that Mary O'Hara would have done this if she had the technology, but they are wrong. Just because no-one has ever written about either of them without using the word "ethereal", it doesn't mean that they are in any way related. For Mary, the nuns have a case to answer. For Enya, we salute them. "She would put a horn on a snowman."

FALLON, B.P.

A spiritual advisor to the Government of Rock'n'Roll, Beep's job-description is a nebulous thing. Due to some Druidic method of manoeuvre, he invariably winds up in the entourage of whoever happens to be hot, be it T. Rex, Led Zeppelin, The Boomtown Rats or the Plastic Ono Band, with whom he waved a tambourine on *Top Of The Pops*. A distinguished, um, disc-jockey and rock journalist, he is on, uh, intimate terms with a shocking number of rock legends, living and dead. If John Lennon or

Marc Bolan want a good chinwag about old times, they tune in to Beep on the astral plane. Sometimes they are joined by God, or "The Main Man". Liable to describe sexual intercourse as "the third-leg boogie vibe", he has occasionally been subjected to random violence. On one such occasion, the newspapers failed to coin the obvious headline, "Beep Bopped By Lula". He has been seen receiving Holy Communion.

FAITHFULL, Marianne

She has sought sanctuary among us, and we welcome her, as we would any woman who knows how to enjoy herself. As far as we can glean from her memoirs, Marianne did everything that is bad for you, but then, give anything a lash once, eh? No more than the rest of us, her happiness has Guinness connections.

FARRELL, Brian

In broadcasting as in politics, there are elder statesmen, and this is one of them. The TV series *Farrell* seemed like a good idea, with the gentleman presenter mulling over the great issues at a civilised Sunday pace. So we sit back nursing a post-prandial brandy, expect-

ing to enjoy some cerebral jousting between Brian and, say, Boutros Boutros Ghali, and instead we see Noel Davern. During the high Summer of his career, the feisty academic polished off many a General Election, and the rose in his lapel never wilted, possibly due to the amount of verbal manure coming at it from all angles. You would be left with a nagging feeling that Brian was running the country. And in a way, you know, he was.

See Bowman, John.

FINUCANE, Marian

The mad, the bad, and the dangerous-to-know get their fifteen minutes of fame on her *Live Line* programme. From the ethics of pig-racing to the technicalities of abortion and Sinéad O'Connor's poetry, the patron saint of cranks is there to lend an ear. For this inestimable public service, her callers congratulate her on running a great show. Hell, it is a great show. Marian was mortified to become embroiled in the Mespil Road flats fiasco, during which elderly tenants were worried about being ejected like dogs by rich persons. It was just a little nest-egg for her retirement, and she lives on a farm, where the cattle don't ring her up every time they get annoyed about something. People are surprised at how tall she is.

Fitzgerald, Eithne

Elected with a massive vote, she has grappled with Ethics in Government in a fatalistic sort of way, knowing she is backing a loser, but going along for the ride as her Fianna Fail partners yelp their indignation. Unlike them, she has not known hardship.

FITZGERALD, Frances

During her time as head of the Council for the Status of Women, it became better known as the Council for the Women of Status, with Frances eventually deciding that she could best advance the struggle by becoming a Fine Gael TD. This was feminism-in-sensible-shoes, but then the Party was still getting over Twink. If she has anything unusual to say, it has yet to be said. Perhaps she is waiting until something unusual happens.

FITZGERALD, Dr. Garret

"Apart from a very tentative approach I received in late 1975 — which I rejected because of my commitment to the Northern Ireland problem — this is the first time that the name of an Irish candidate for the post of President of the European Commission has been seriously considered internationally." Dr.Fitzgerald wrote this in the *Irish Times*, referring to the career prospects of his ample-bottomed friend, "Bunter" Sutherland. His finances may have stalled with the GPA catastrophe, but his vanity remains undimmed. Bred to rule, he cultivated an avuncular image in contrast to the nouveau riche Haughey. An unhealthy fascination with air and rail timetables marked him as an absent-minded sort of chap with a well-concealed addiction to political bloodsport. As he surveys the wreckage of

47

48

the economy, the "constitutional crusade" and the Anglo-Irish Agreement from a lofty distance, he pens intimidating newspaper columns with the word "Europe" in the headline. His grey eminence develops, but his hair has become more manageable.

See Prendergast, Peter; Sutherland, Peter.

FLYNN, Padraig

Many hours of grooming by Carr Communications have failed to extract the essence of Pee, which is forever that of the headmaster about to ask you whether you have your sums done. Strictly neanderthal on "social issues" within the national territory, in Brussels he became Red Pee, arguing for fair work practices and the rights of women, which were matters on which he had been hitherto totally silent. Many believe that he hoisted Mary Robinson to the Presidency with an attack on her newly discovered family values. The mind boggles at his intercourse with Unionists during negotiations. "Pee" often refers to himself in the third person, as though he is powerless to intervene in the destiny of Pee Flynn. There was an absolutely hilarious suggestion that he should hand over his Commissioner's chair so that the ample-bottomed "Bunter" Sutherland could run Europe instead. He is happy to be called The Messiah, and once told the present writer that he is "not big into heavy rock".

See Prone, Terry.

FOX, Johnny

A Wicklow Protestant, he holds trenchant

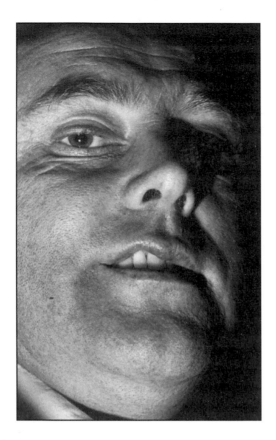

views on homosexuals and homosexuality. Yeah, verily, he stands up for the Protestant right to condemn gays and indeed whoever else takes their fancy. Clearly, if Johnny *fox* any-one, it certainly won't be a chap. He has spoken of the need for a man to "take a wife." But where? That is the question.

See Ross, Shane; Boothman, Jack.

FRIDAY, Gavin

Surrealist, songwriter, and restaurateur, he lives on the shadowy end of the Cabaret scene, where the busses don't run. Founder of the Virgin Prunes and the Blue Jaysus Club, he has yet to disport himself on *Play The Game* as is his right. The chameleon Friday raises the banal to the sublime, making Bingo hip at Mr. Pussy's cafe, which he oversees with the more conservative drag-artist, Mister Pussy. When his old mucker Bono wants to chill out and talk to a regular guy, he talks to Gavin, the salt of the earth if not quite the heart of the rowel.

FRIEL, Brian

The great man must enjoy the drama which ensues when he writes one of his rare duds,

50

and the secret society of theatre-goers make their excuses. In *Sunday World*, they make their excuses and leave. In the Drama Department of the *Irish Times*, it becomes "challenging" and "worthy of a second viewing", but never a dud. One of the foremost playwrights of the 20th century, his shyness of publicity has made him almost completely unknown to the general public. Eventually they will toast him in pubs named after him.

FRISBEE, Mai

A quare name but great stuff.
See Burke-Kennedy, Mary Elizabeth; Stewart-Liberty, Nell.

FOX, The Border

Leader of the kidnap gang which seized the dentist John O'Grady, he became one of those terrorists who is accorded a nickname, due to their alarming enthusiasm for the lifestyle. Doubt was cast on his motivation when it was alleged that the O'Grady ransom was required less for the funding of the armed struggle, than for a new life in Australia. Bondi Beach will have to wait. He languishes in Portlaoise Gaol.

FUREY, Finbarr

"I taught Liam O'Flynn everything he knows. But I didn't teach him everything I know." That's Finbarr for you, always having the craic. His buddy Billy Connolly recalls meeting the Fureys when it looked as though they had just learned how to walk upright. Always having the craic.

GALLAGHER, Patrick

It is far more difficult to blow a family fortune than this man made it look. He cut a few deals too many and became very poor almost over lunch, bringing a fair few innocents with him. Having studied his methods, the experts decided that he had to go to jail. This is also much more difficult than it looks for a man in his position, who once led in a winner at Ascot. Free at last, he has brought his talents to Africa.

GALLAGHER, Rory

Ror-ee, Ror-ee, Ror-ee, Ror-ee! Oh how we boogied as our first true guitar hero belted out the blues on those nights of magic at the Stadium. The Germans loved him too, and used to shout Ror-ee, Ror-ee, Ror-ee, Ror-ee, in German. "Did you ever wake up with those bullfrogs on your mind?", he would holler. We sure did, still wearing our lumberjack shirts, just like Rory.

GARLAND, Roger

The first Green TD was also a Lloyd's "name" (ha, ha, ha, ha, ha) and an opponent of Divorce. This kind of thing is confusing for the voters, and eventually they saw some sort of personality deficit in Roger. "He is his own man."

GAVIN, Frankie

De Danann's virtuoso fiddler can make it talk in every language under the sun. I was told by a man who went to Heaven once that when he arrived, and went looking for God, he saw this musical session in progress, featuring such wizards as Jimi Hendrix, Miles Davis, Pablo Casals and Frankie Gavin. "Jaysus, there's Frankie," he said, immediately feeling at home.

But St. Peter put him right. "Actually, that's God," he said, "He just thinks that he's Frankie Gavin."

GELDOF, Bob

He just wants to write pop songs, and they can't let him forget that he saved the world. In saving the world, he inadvertently saved the careers of countless reprobates who now owe their success to his raising of the global consciousness via satellite. Prior to this, most pillars of the Irish establishment thought that he was a complete scumbag and a degenerate and a braggart. The feeling was mutual. They still think along these lines, but it is not in their interest to admit it.

GEOGHEGAN-QUINN, Maire

She was a woman in politics before it became fashionable, but somehow, being a Fianna Fail woman made her a member of some third gender. Her chromosomes had been stamped with the FF motif, so she could pass as one of the lads. She was handsome, capable, and there weren't too many of her. "That lassie will go far," the elders would yelp. And how right they were.

GILES, John

Though revered by all of us as a great player, there are some curmudgeons who refuse to elevate him to the pantheon, due to the studs still embedded in their shins from his Leeds days. Laser-like in the precision of his match-analysis, he thinks and talks a beautiful game. In his playing days, we all called him "Johnny". Isn't it strange then, that his brother-in-law Nobby Stiles never became Nob Stiles? Perhaps not.

See Dunphy, Eamon.

GILLIS, Alan

For people unfamiliar with the fine print of the CAP (and there are some), the highlight of his Presidency of the IFA was the invasion of the Department of Agriculture by a flock of sheep. Something to do with Maaaaaaaaastricht, no doubt. As an MEP, he must be more formal. Strasbourg does not share our sense of humour in these matters.

GINNITY, Noel V.

Being the subject of a *Late Late Show* Special and the victim of a kidnap drama, he is a member of two elite groupings. Noted for his acerbic view of the political classes, he leaves funny greetings on his answering machine, like

"Paddy Clarke, Ha, Ha, Ha, Emmett Stagg, ha,ha,ha,ha, Bertie Ahern, ha, ha, ha, ha, ha", and so on. He gave up The Drink before it gave him up.

GOGAN, Larry

He became immortalised throughout much of the English-speaking world via the works of Roddy Doyle, who named the Rabbitte family dog "Larrygogan". The turntable king still retains his remarkable enthusiasm for Pop, though by the disposable standards of the genre, he is approximately 40,000 years old, his age verifiable only by radiocarbon dating. Then again, so is Mick Jagger, the only difference being that Larry still has his dignity. As regards his notorious 60-second quiz, perhaps the most remarkable thing was not that a contestant sited the vertebrae in the head, but that she emerged the winner.

GOODMAN, Larry

The cattle baron was a good friend to the democratic process, contributing large sums to at least three political parties. Never let it be said that he courted favouritism. He fell foul of the less-than-democratic Saddam Hussein, who took his beef and forgot to pay for it. The taxpayer was happy to oblige in the national interest — which, happily, coincided with the Goodman interest. Reports of massive irregularities at some of his plants led to the Beef Tribunal, at which the wholly ridiculous suggestion was made that Larry might have a clue about selling 14-year-old steaks to the Arabs,

or getting them into bad odour with Mohammed by fiddling with the labels. In fact, it was all the fault of Susan O'Keeffe, a television journalist. How could it be otherwise?
See O'Keeffe, Susan.

GRACE, Brendan

He has touched a resonant chord among his compatriots with his skill at pretending to be drunk, and his understanding of the fact that drunk people are usually trying to pretend to be sober. Hardened observers such as Donie Cassidy and Frank Sinatra consider him to be world-class, and the American corporate sector has taken him to its wallet. He can be vulgar without being obscene.

GREENE, Philip

"And the embattled Hoops are strapped to the mast as wave after wave of Spaniards roll over them." Whether describing the oranges of Seville becoming bitter lemons for the boys in green, or a fire breaking out in the "Press Box" at St. Mel's Park, Athlone, Philip gave it oodles of welly. His flow was staunched on one occasion when we lost him behind the Iron Curtain after he joked about a player being sent to Siberia for his sins. The KGB knew that they were dealing with a maestro, the West was the best, and their act was doomed. When he returned, all our bitter lemons became oranges again.

GUERIN, Orla

She has shown expansionist tendencies, emerging from the RTE newsroom to bestride

the wreckage of Eastern Europe, and then bidding for domination of the West with her ill-starred attempt to join the European Parliament. Journalism did not provide her with the scope to accomplish her goals. For most journalists, this is not a problem. They can accomplish their "goals" in Lillie's Bordello. She wanted more.

GUILBAUD, Patrick

Paddy by name, French by nature, the renowned restaurateur is almost part of what we are. He has wielded a mean cleaver for the gentry, and added a dash of sophistication to our busy lives. As the old Irish saying goes, *"is fearr na Francaigh ins an gcistin"*, or "every kitchen needs a Frenchman."

HALL, Frank

His Hall's *Pictorial Weekly* is fondly remembered for its mild political satire. Conor Cruise O'Brien felt that it undermined the Cosgrave junta and, ever since, RTE has welcomed political satire the way that rabbits embrace myxomatosis. For his services to the nation, Hall got to see loads of dirty films, and censor them. He has watched Liam Cosgrave and Linda Lovelace going down, the ingredients of a rich and varied life.

HAMILTON, George

The man for whom the word "feisty" might have been specifically coined, his commentaries can get a bit too feisty when the Republic take the lead. The more George enthuses about the masterful dominance of the Green Machine, the more we howl at the screen to deflate his hubris. There have been amusing rivalries between himself and Jimmy Magee over who mans the microphone for prestige matches, but this need not concern any sane person.

See Green, Philip; Magee, Jimmy.

HAMILTON, Judge

At a stage of his life when he might have been looking forward to more pleasant things, he was handed the Chair of the Beef Tribunal. Exploring the mysteries of boning-halls and the myriad delights of Intervention, he may well have re-appraised that account at F.X. Buckley. When he suggested to Mr. Reynolds that he (Reynolds) appeared to listen to the best advice available, and then do different, the then Taoiseach reckoned that he was spot on. The Report contained something for everyone, a Selection Box for the Irish Establishment. They were tired but happy.

HANAFIN, Des

He drank like a fish, he organised the finances of Fianna Fáil, but it was a road accident which put him back on his feet in a big way. His tireless services to Catholicism won him the equestrian Knight of St.Gregory award, and now he rides to the defence of the unborn

and the unhappily married, brandishing the torch of Rome. His hero is Padre Pio, noted for his powers of bi-location, a quality which is highly regarded in Fianna Fáil circles. He disagrees with Norman Tebbitt's view that human life begins when you get a job. It begins at the moment of conception, according to Des. Forget about the guilt-free fuck with this chap.

HANLY, David

"Have you partaken of the moist red gland?," the *Morning Ireland* man asked an excited David Norris on Bloomsday. For this, he is immortal. His stentorian tones can induce a feeling of Mourning Ireland which is completely fitting in the cir-cumstances. When brother Mick hit paydirt on the song-writing front, David became "Mick Hanly's brother", where once Mick had been his brother. He is the only RTE celebrity who can be seen reading a book in public. It is thought that he reads in pri-vate, too.

HARDIMAN, Adrian

A leading member of the IRB, the Inordinately Rich Barristers association, he achieved nationwide notoriety after a contretemps in the Shelbourne Hotel involving his fellow IRB man, Gerry Danaher. He forgave his colleague and friend because the remarks were made "in drink". A liberal-minded man, he is always ready to appear on RTE for some legal and gynaecological argy-bargy with the forces of Pro-Life darkness. He usually wins, but then the Pro-Lifers would expect little more from such a Dublin Four pup. "Would you listen to that pup?," they say.
See Danaher, Gerry.

HARNEY, Mary

There is no smog in Dublin any more, thanks to Mary, who accomplished this with Padraig Flynn allegedly hiding behind her skirts. An incredible achievement all round. Now she is Mother of all the Progressive Democrats, her heart broken when the precocious Pat Cox and Martin Cullen enraged the family by setting up their own political businesses in opposition to her. She must now understand why Fianna Fail considered PDs to be motherfuckers from day one.

HARRINGTON, Paul

Talented singer-songwriter, he won the Eurovision with as much dignity as he could muster, acting as warm-up man for the astonishing 'Riverdance'. His recovery from Eurovision has been understandably slow, but his general health is thought to be excellent.

See Logan, Johnny.

HARRIS, Eoghan

Some time around March 1972, Eoghan Harris went into his local newsagent, where he pur-

chased a number of papers and periodicals, and a packet of cigarettes. He exchanged some pleasantries about the day that was in it, and received the change of a ten-pound note from the shop assistant. Then he went home. This is the only uncontroversial thing that Eoghan Harris has ever done. But he probably wasn't thinking straight at the time, and would do it all differently now.

HARRIS, Richard

The thinking man's Oliver Reed, it must be said that actors were a lot more fun in the era of Harris and Peter O'Toole and Richard Burton. They were like rock'n'roll stars, great men for being totally drunk in public, wrecking pubs, hotels, marriages, and themselves, with equal aplomb, always with a bit of Shakespeare to justify it to the vulgarians. Where have all the hellraisers gone? Compared to Harris and all of

that wild bunch on the Celtic fringe, Sean Penn
is just a big girl's blouse. You know that he
doesn't mean it.

HAUGHEY, Charles J.

The charismatic and highly-sexed Haughey
spawned a whole new species known as the
"Charlie Man", a creature utterly devoted to the
fuehrer throughout his topsy-turvy career.
From the Arms Trial, through the wilderness
years consuming rubber chicken in vast quan-

tities, and on to the GUBU era, the "Charlie Man" kept the faith. They took a roguish delight in his accumulation of wealth as though by magic, reasoning that if he could do so well for himself, perhaps he could keep "the country" in funds as well. Napoleonic in stature and gesture, his effigy in Donie Cassidy's Wax Museum is taller than actual size in order to create a more statesmanlike stance next to Garret Fitzgerald, who doubted his pedigree. Sayings include, "there are some fuckers whose throats you'd like to cut, and throw them off the edge of a fucking cliff," and "no, no, no." See Mara, P.J.; Fitzgerald, Garret; Haughey, Sean; See everyone.

HAUGHEY, Sean

He has attempted to carve out a role distinct from that of his illustrious sire by growing a ludicrous moustache and making asinine noises about the "silent majority", and their alleged misgivings about the "liberal agenda". Kids, they say the darnedest things.
See Haughey, Charles J.

HEALY, Shay

A very difficult man to pin down to any one discipline in the industry of human happiness. Off-hand, the only thing that Shay has not done as an all-round entertainer is to crash a light aeroplane into the White House. With his restless creativity, he has a permanent ticket for The Sweep.

HEALY-RAE, Jackie

In a Party notorious for its absurdist hair-dos,

63

the Fianna Fail councillor from Kilgarvan has sported a particularly fearsome tonsure. In the heat of Árd-Fheis battle, it resembled liquid tar poured onto the skull. He once appeared on RTE television speaking from the Cork studio, wearing a Russian-style hat, like Elton John waiting for a hair transplant to "take". A "Charlie Man".

See Cassidy, Donie.

HEANEY, Seamus

Our greatest living sit-down poet, he located the academic clitoris of America and Britain with his turf-strewn stanzas. Criticised by Desmond Fennell for his failure to produce a memorable, ringing verse or two about the nationalist condition, he will still appear on *Up For The Match* to talk about Gaelic football, reassuring us that he hasn't lost the run of himself. Bucolic though this is, it is something of a relief from the goddamn poetry. What's it all about, Seamus?

HEDERMAN, Carmencita

Sam G. Smyth put it thus: "If the neck of Carmencita Hederman was rendered down to its base elements, there would be sufficient brass to make bedsteads for a dozen king-sized models, and enough of the non-ferrous material left over to make candelabra which would illuminate the new Croke Park complex." For shame. An incredibly popular Lord Mayor of Dublin during Millenium year, her profile plummeted after she made a forlorn bid for the Presidential nomination, leaving the way open for Mrs. Robinson to become Queen of

Ireland, with Carmencita in exile somewhere in the bowels of leafy Dublin Four. Titles ruled out for her autobiography include "The Wrong Side of the Tracks" and "My Struggle."

HEGARTY, Dermot

He scored one of the biggest hits in County'n'Irish history with '21 Years'. The public warmed to this wholly depressing tale of a person being sentenced to a lengthy jail term in the notorious Dartmoor, without even his mother for company. It may be the most depressing song ever written, but it seemed to capture the spirit of the time. There was much to be depressed about.

See Cassidy, Donie; Stuart, Gene; Daniels, Roly; Tom, Big.

HEWSON, Paul

Singer, songwriter, publican, restaurateur, niteclub owner, and collector of fine houses, "Bono" is, above all, a family man. As Lloyd Bentsen might have put it, "I know Adam Clayton, I served with Adam Clayton, and Bono, you are no Adam Clayton." Or is he? There is a bit of the devil about "Bono", and to demonstrate that his reputation as a God-botherer is somewhat exaggerated, he will say "fuck" on American television. Worse, if they'd let him. U2's enormous legion of American fans may have prevented "Bono" from displaying the wicked sense of humour which he undoubtedly possesses, and most certainly needs for the job. They wouldn't get it. He knows Jack Nicholson.

HICKEY, Tom

No matter how far the gifted thespian travels into the avant garde, the surreal, and the downright "difficult", he will forever be Benjy Riordan to the people of Middle Ireland. "Isn't Benjy great at the acting all the same?", they will say, as he interprets Tom McIntyre's latest masterpiece. "I hope the ould fella finds out about this," they will say, as it all becomes too difficult. He bears his Cross like a man.

See McIntyre, Tom.

HIGGINS, Michael D.

How sharper than a serpent's tooth is the ingratitude of the punter. For decades, people had been bellyaching about the nitwits, balubas, and philistines who worm their way into Ministerial Mercs. Then a man who admits to reading a book or two without moving his lips becomes Minister For Fun, and they're queueing up to jeer at his poetry. Like the Church's approach to homosexuality, Art is only acceptable in a politician if he doesn't practise it. Michael D. is the first Minister in the history of the state to use words like "holistic" in public. (The other bastards think that holistic is a way of describing the state of the roads in Cavan.) Dessie O'Malley thought that he would "go mad" in government. Instead, Dessie went mad out of Government.

HILLERY, Dr. Patrick

"Ye can have Boland, but ye can't have Fianna Fail," he howled from an Ard-Fheis platform. Ah, the agony of choice. In more tranquil times, he signed us up for "Europe", and later lived for some fourteen years in Áras An Uachtaráin, guarding the Constitution — an almost totally uneventful period enlivened only by the odd mysterious phone call from Party colleagues, and the visit of the Pope. By playing golf incessantly, he moved the Presidency towards the American style.

HOGAN, Des

The extravagantly talented writer told an interviewer (me) that he had lost two novels. A gust of wind blew one of them into the Grand Canal, and the other one went missing somewhere in Iowa after a bacchanalian evening to mark its completion. It was ironic, then, that Ballinasloe's greatest wordsmith was living for a while in Lewisham in a building which housed the chairperson of EXIT, the organisation which assists people into easeful death, should they so desire. Still with us, he has many surviving works to his credit, and travels widely.

HOOLEY, Terri

One-eyed supremo of the great Good Vibrations record label, Terri is responsible for the most worthwhile coming together of the different traditions in the North in the entire history of that province. Sure, they are brought together under various guises to "get to know one another", but they don't make records like 'Teenage Kicks', 'Big Time', 'Right Way Home', or 'You're A Disease'. In punk rock, the colour of your religion had no meaning, and Terri did a lot to make it happen. None of the North's leading politicians has ever heard of him, because they are too ignorant.

HOUGHTON, Ray

Little Razor was behind the two most hair-raising hours in recent Irish memory, with his early goals against England and Italy. Score early and often, Ray, like they vote in the West. "Who put the ball in the England net? I did," he sang, marking the end of 800 years of slavery and revenge for Skibbereen. You would hardly notice that he is Scottish until he speaks.

HOULIHAN, Con

The colossal Castle Islander has expanded the frontiers of sportswriting to include lyrical meditations on turf, wildlife, public transport, politics, angling, education and marmalade. "Any man who can put an apostrophe in the wrong place is capable of anything," says Con, who is himself capable of wearing an anorak in the mid-day sun of Mexico City or Las Vegas. When the President of UCC, Dr. Alfred O'Rahilly, expressed the hope that the new graduates would follow in their fathers' footsteps, Con declared that he was following in his father's trousers. Reputed to have played rugby in his bare feet, his legend is such that people ask him for his autograph at football

matches. Essentially a shy man, his yearning for privacy is not helped by his resemblance to a section of Mount Rushmore. His greatness is assured.

HOWLIN, Brendan

A pocket rocket and a "safe pair of hands", simultaneously, it is rather charming to think of him, a Government Minister, still living with his mother. They are occasionally visited by members of the neo-nazi Youth Defence, brandishing photographs of foetuses, and attempting to implicate Brendan in the slaughter of the innocents. He has been pictured topless at a rock concert, something which could never be said of Government Ministers such as Frank Aiken or Sean McBride.

HUGHES, Sean

Comedian and poet, he has enchanted Channel 4 viewers with his tales from the North London lager belt, and his existential musings. One of our leading young emigrants, he could never have become rich and famous in Ireland, because RTE has a strict policy of discrimination against funny people. He jokes that his father never hugged him, because basically, he didn't like him.

HUME, John

His ceaseless struggle to elucidate the nationalist viewpoint has led him to neglect more mundane matters, such as his hairstyle. One is given to suspect that he is homeless, as he appears to spend most of his life in television studios, availing of the free light and heat, and surviving on morsels of complimentary food. Such self-sacrifice has captured the heart of our Government, which does whatever he says, regardless of how often he says it. Sayings include "peace-in-a-week" and "two balls of roasted snow".

HURLEY, Red

This "hunk" brought new levels of sophistication to the Irish Cabaret scene. Those with ears to hear thought that he was nearly as good as any American singer, and could make it big over there. His slow lift-off Stateside can only be attributed to the fact that his Christian name suggested Communist leanings, and that when promoters heard the name "Red" Hurley, they immediately thought, "there goes a running-dog lackey of Stalin and Kruschkev, taking his orders directly from the Kremlin." Nothing could be further from the truth.

HUSSEY, Gemma

She invited us into the vortex of power with her Cabinet memoirs. Exciting times they were too, by all accounts. She was featured on the cover of *Magill* magazine, but the interview inside was printed without recourse to capital letters, in the style of e e cummings, the goddamn poet. Despite this uncharacteristic lapse of Vincent Browne's organ into the avant garde, the magazine ceased publication shortly afterwards.

INGOLDSBY, Pat

If he finds that a person is boring him, he tells them straight out. This is a very brave policy for a poet to pursue. Pat has overcome many difficulties to become a much-loved writer of idiosyncratic verse and prose, and a star of children's television. He writes his poems in comprehensible English, the better that we might understand what the fuck he is talking about. On adult television. he has spoken the word "vagina", with some deliberation. He disputed his neighbour's right to possess a monkey.

IRELAND, John De Courcy

The ancient mariner and socialist is more entitled than most to be synonymous with Ireland, as there are times when he can appear like the only decent human being in the entire country. He has shown us where the sea is, what it's like, and how we might utilise it if we were interested in that sort of thing. Which we are not, really.

JORDAN, Eddie

He had a dream that Ireland would take her rightful place at the top of Formula One racing. And so it came to pass. Fast Eddie was completely undaunted by the fact that Ireland has of course no rightful place within an asses roar of Formula One racing. But he did it anyway. It is a dramatic example of what you can achieve if you can persuade people to give you twenty million dollars a year.

JORDAN, Neil

Like the motor-racing Jordan, Neil has found that it is easier to persuade foreigners to give you millions of dollars than to extract the nec-

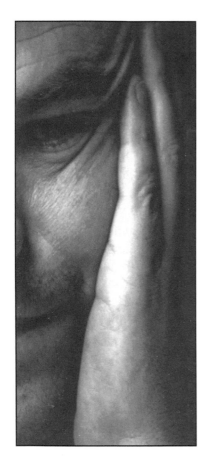

essary funds from Irish people. Perhaps they don't have it. Perhaps they are just mean and stupid. There are those who resent his Oscar-winning *The Crying Game* being described as British, just because it was made with British money. They have their shite. A writer of sublime prose as well as a daring film-maker, Neil is a real live genius. As he grows older, he looks increasingly vulpine.

KEANE, John B.

His contribution to public order has been immense, as his plays have kept thousands indoors on the long nights after Samhain, exorcising their frustrations through amateur dramatics, when they might be fomenting revolution instead. The critics are coming round to an appreciation of John B. by discovering things about his plays which he hadn't the wit to put in himself. He is probably the only great living dramatist who is also a licensed vintner, a duality which hones his instinct for getting bums on seats. But you don't have to leave his plays if you get too pissed. John B. would talk the hind legs off a donkey, and the donkey would bray for more. The "B" stands for "B".

KEANE, Moss

Hard as nails, tough as teak, Moss trampled the thin line between rugby and agriculture, and took very few prisoners along the way. The Geneva Convention was set to one side

when Moss was on the case. We believed that there was no other way. He is a Civil Servant.

See McBride, Willie John.

KEANE, Roy

Hard as nails, tough as teak, he is known to his United clubmates as "Damien", because "there's a bit of the Devil in him." Roy's weekly stipend could conceivably send the entire population of his native Mayfield to the Cote d'Azur for a month, but they'd probably miss the Leeside craic. Having submitted himself to the timeless ritual of altercations in nite-clubs, he is now a mature International Footballer, playing a blinder in the World Cup, while upholding his principles by refusing to score. "He has a great engine."

KEANE, Terry

Hard as nails, tough as teak, the comparisons with her namesake Moss end here, because Terry is "one of Ireland's most beautiful women," while Moss is a big, ugly, corporation of a Kerryman. A "Charlie Woman" through and through, she reports the activities of the rich and glamourous in her witty newspaper column, while remaining somehow above it all. About two inches above it all. Men worship her, women envy her, as she brings a dash of elegance into their drab lives. For the ordinary readers, she supplies an indispensable public service by keeping them abreast of current trends on the Manhattan luxury hotel scene, or the price of bullshot in Barbados.

KEELY, Dermot

Hard as nails, tough as teak, the much-travelled League of Ireland defender took as few prisoners as Moss Keane in his own way. As a manager, he complained of the intense pressure on clubs to stay in the higher echelons. He forecast that the day would come when the administrators would be trying to attract the crowds with live human sacrifices. Others felt that in Dermot's time, that day had already been.

KEATING, Bil

Whe hi nam appear o th credit a th en o a RT televisio programm, peopl wonde wh h spell Bil wit on "l". That hi busines.

KEATING, Justin

Like many another, he was under the impression that the Seventies would be Socialist. Instead, the Seventies were elephant flares, platform shoes, gold medallions, The Bay City Rollers, Slade, Suzi Quatro, and Mud, jazz fusion, triple-live albums, 30-minute drum solos, Ted Nugent, and eventually punk rock. He still became a Government Minister, but the electorate grew tired of that, and now he is a journalist with a reputation as an outstanding cook. Come the new Millennium, the Socialist will be seventy.

KEARNEY, Richard

Easily our most handsome philosopher, he

might be more at home in France, where intellectuals are considered sexy even if they look like beasts. In euphoric mood on the election of President Robinson, he wrote an hilarious poem telling the women of Ireland that he loved them. First the Pope, now Richard Kearney. Things were looking up. He founded the deeply serious *Crane Bag* periodical, and people who thought that they liked poetry suddenly realised that they knew nothing about it at all. They were better off.

KEENAN, Brian

It was good to think of him living quietly in the West of Ireland, getting his head together after the horrors of Beirut. The beauty of the landscape was as therapeutic as the fact that he was extremely unlikely to encounter much in the line of Islam. He could also drink all the drink in the world, as promised, but would have his work cut out making love to all the women in the world as also promised. He probably thought better of that anyway.

KEOGH, John

Here is one man who clearly had a high old time in the '60s, because he has spent much of his subsequent career re-living it, through his band Full Circle, and by excavating the archives in RTE to remind us of Dickie Rock and Brendan Bowyer sending them home sweating. His efforts help to explain the widespread desire to experiment with drugs at that time.

KELLY, Eamonn

Masterful actor and storyteller. It is interesting to imagine "In My Father's Time" fifty years hence. "Well, Matty produced the oul' marching powder and laid it out on the mirror as straight as the lines of a railway track. 'The land of Colombia is rich and bountiful', says he, rolling up a ten-pound note and snorting half of South America up his right nostril. 'Courage!', said Kelleher, taking a big fat bamboozler from behind his ear and raising the roof with a blast of Prince, who was very big in that locality. It was then that the craic started in earnest."

KELLY, Gary

The brilliant young full-back surprised even himself by scoring against Germany, and by having young women scream his name in public. With disarming honesty, he spoke of watching Italia '90 in Drogheda, a bit under the influence, at fifteen. But this didn't surprise anyone who knows anything about Drogheda. Or about being fifteen.

KELLY, Henry

It is astonishing to think that Henry was once a remarkably serious human being. Far from the Pro-Celebrity Golf circuit he was reared, when he swanned through UCD matching wits with the greatest minds of his generation, and held the Chair of Northern Studies at the *Irish Times*. With alarming ease, he transformed himself into a professional Irishman, making his fortune by generally acting the bollocks on a variety of embarrassing TV shows. He became a radio disc-jockey, playing classical music for people who don't like classical music. He did it all, and he did it smiling. No cultural snob he.

KELLY, Seán

"The Beast" is arguably our greatest ever sporting legend, because he achieved it all in a foreign language, and without being particularly friendly. He was civil enough in his own way, was Seán, but hardly a font of bonhomie. From the mouth of Kelly, "super" sounded like a veiled criticism. "He did his talking in the saddle."

See Roche, Stephen.

KENNEDY, Geraldine

A very serious journalist indeed, Sean Doherty thought she was so serious that he had her phone tapped. She received £20,000 in compensation, and that was serious too. Something in the air led her to take the serious step of becoming a Progressive Democrat TD. At the whim of the electorate, she returned to journalism, and the Chair of Politics at the *Irish Times.* Though her political allegiance had been made clear, a serious journalist such as Geraldine would not allow any bias to colour her reporting. Or anything else either.

KENNEDY, Tom

Alias Tom

KENNELLY, Brendan

Callers to a radio phone-in nominated him the sexiest man in Ireland, even though he writes poems. But there were good Germans and there are good poets. It is his voice, apparently, which does the trick, a voice known throughout the land as a result of Kennelly's astonishing performances on Toyota ads. It is refreshing to hear a man of such intellect engaging with the mundanities of Japanese cars. One has difficulty imagining Seamus Heaney telling us to hurry, hurry, hurry, down to Crazy Prices.

KENNY, Mary

In recent times, certain women have discovered that a good way of becoming a columnist with a posh English paper is to slag the hell out of feminism. Mary was the pioneer in this uncharted land, entertaining the upper classes with what Julie Burchill described as the worldview of a Mexican peasant woman. Mary was a particularly prize catch for conservatives, having inflated condoms in public with her own wind. It was like a KGB colonel defecting to the West, declaring that it was all a cod. She is under the impression that cosmopolitan West Cork is in "rural Ireland".

KENNY, Pat

If RTE was a football team, Pat would have played in every position, including goalkeeper. He is dismayed that most people he meets think that he is richer than he actually is. Not only is he less rich than Gay Byrne, he is not even as rich as Pat Kenny. His *Kenny Live* programme demonstrates his eerie versatility, with its mixture of chatter, fun and games, leading into an interview with someone who

has had his head chopped off and sewn back on again. "We have a really great show for you tonight," he says. How can he tell?

KENNY, Tony

Noel Pearson looked at Tony Kenny, oozing class, and decided that here was the man to play Jesus Christ Almighty during his Superstar phase. Biblical scholars were unable to suspend their disbelief, but Kenny still doesn't look a day over 33. For the American tourists at Jury's cabaret, each Supper might be their last.

See Pearson, Noel.

KILANIN, Lord

He held what is undoubtedly the best job in the entire world, President of the International Olympic Committee. Members of the IOC basically have to travel the world in magnificent style, meeting people who will do literally anything for their vote. It didn't change His Lordship. He had always lived well, even in Oughterard.

KILCOYNE, Fr. Colm

Successor to Fr. Nash S.J. as the priestly columnist in the *Sunday Press*, he is more

"with it" than old Nash, whose copy allegedly drove a Press operative to threaten self-immolation if he was not relieved from its stewardship. His *Sunday World* rival, Fr. Brian D'Arcy, loves to laugh. Fr. Colm is not quite so gay. But he likes to laugh, all the same.
See D'Arcy, Fr. Brian; Casey, Bishop.

KILCOYNE, Louis

Currently exploring the mysteries of FIFA politics, this ambitious football administrator transformed Glenmalure Park, home of Shamrock Rovers, into an attractive housing development. Furious fans have dubbed him "The Man Who Sold The World."

KILLELEA, Mark

"Markeen" has been identified as "the face of Fianna Fáil". If aliens required a photo-fit of the species, it is thought that the super-cute Galwayman's visage would tell them all they wanted to know. A committed European, he tries to bring a little bit of Brussels to the heart of the West. Bon appetit, Mark Killelea.

KILKENNY, Osmund

Accountant to the stars, by definition "Ossie" exercises a huge creative influence on our popular culture. The rock'n'roll number-cruncher may be the only man alive who knows how much money U2 have. This is such a sobering thought that he never takes alcohol.
See McGuinness, Paul.

KINANE, Michael

The champion jockey resisted the temptation

to base himself in England, deciding instead to win all the big races on spare rides. Mick has only to place his posterior on the stable's second string, and it becomes a winged Pegasus. He has not escaped the puzzling new phenomenon of horses falling on the Flat.

KING, Adele

In common with Eva Peron, Glenda Jackson and Melina Mercouri, "Twink" fused showbiz with politics, striking a near-mortal blow to Fine Gael by performing a sketch at their Árd-Fheis. The vivacious comedienne has also ventured into the fields of law and property, with her mortgage repayments becoming a topic of national controversy. She is bound to agree that there is no business like showbusiness.

Those with long memories recall her as a child star with Maxi, Dick, and Twink. But they can't recall Dick, no matter how they try.

KINSELLA, Sean

Ireland's first celebrity chef made his Mirabeau restaurant a place of legend wherein Demis Roussos would consume a gross of oysters and forty steaks at the one sitting, or the James Last Orchestra would eat a whole cow. Famous for its big bills,

81

the party drew to a close when the taxman submitted his.

See Last, James.

KITT, Tom

As the least ugly member of the Cabinet, he became a sort of Minister For Women, in the absence of a suitable woman for the post. He is considered to be "young", and "not very ugly."

KNOWLES, Sonny

The velvet voice, the snow-white hair, the winning smile, it can mean only one thing: you are watching afternoon television, and Sonny wants you to sing along with the toon that he is crooning. His relaxed, romantic, style has made him particularly popular with the elderly, the unwell and Joe Duffy. He'll take care of your cares, should you so desire.

LALLY, Mick

As Miley from *Glenroe,* he created a likable agricultural role model, a farmer you could trust. The thoughts of Miley are long, long, thoughts, as he reflects on the Berlin Wall coming down and its impact on the growers of Co. Wicklow, or comes to terms with Biddy's gynaecological needs. Is he happy? Well, he is not "extra happy". Soon, he might be vexed again. But not extra vexed.

LAMBERT, Eugene

The veteran puppeteer brought us *Wanderly Wagon* before video games and all that crap. This RTE vehicle housed such characters as the half-witted O'Brien, the reliable Rory, the omniscient Godmother, Mr. Crow, Foxy Loxy, and the immortal Judge. It was all we had.

LAST, James

He became part of what we are for a while, his Orchestra fashioning the classic hits of Erin into something rather lush and grand. The begrudgers had their say, as always: "What's the difference between the James Last Orchestra and a bull? A bull has the horns out front and the asshole at the back." For shame.

LEAHY, Dr. Paddy

The iconoclastic doctor has accompanied women to England for abortions, and regarded contraception as a viable option for the poor. Dr. Paddy has tried to take religion out of medicine, while many of his colleagues go the opposite way. The bastards.

LEE, Professor Joe

His monumental work, *Ireland 1912-1985, Politics And Society* merged the genres of history and horror, as he documented our exceptional inability to provide for ourselves. Perhaps it would all have been different if smart people like Professor Joe had been running the country, instead of writing big books about the gobshites who wrecked it.

LENIHAN, Brian

Eternally optimistic, Brian was a spin-doctor before the concept was coined, whipping up an Ard-Fheis frenzy, or predicting vast majorities for Fianna Fáil in view of the sheer excellence of all the candidates. Just when he was about to retire to Áras An Uachtaráin with a resounding mandate and a brand new liver, his legend grew even greater, and the gaiety of the nation knew no bounds, as he delivered his "mature reflection" classic on RTE. It sounds like the title of a Phil Coulter album, but Brian's needle was a bit rusty. In victory or defeat, a bloody star.

LEONARD, Hugh

The pro's pro, he was famously described as the only man in Ireland who has become embittered by success. His conspicuous enjoyment of fine foods and wines would seem to give the lie to this. He appears to have seen every "fillum" ever made, and memorised them all down to the last frame. Somehow he has found the spare time to produce a mountain of plays, TV dramas, newspaper articles, and the odd book about cats, but no poems, thank Christ. Such is his dramatist's ability to get people in and out of rooms, he was probably a bouncer in another life.

LISTON, Eoin

The fearsome "Bomber" scored freely for Kerry. Experts agree that he is the greatest bearded Gaelic player of all time.

LOCKE, Josef

The Irish tenor brought a touch of much-needed razzmatazz and vulgarity to his genteel trade. It's been an undulating ride for this '50s superstar. The King of Blackpool seemed to model his career on the town's roller-coaster. He was portrayed with gusto by Ned Beatty in the film *Hear My Song*. Ned was famously butt-fucked by a pair of hillbillies in John Boorman's *Deliverance*. Indeed, were he to play the greatest King Lear in history, chances are that he would still be "the guy who got butt-fucked in *Deliverance*." But he did Josef proud.

LOFTUS, Dr. Mick

Former GAA President, the Mayo County

Coroner is a lonely voice denouncing the culture of drink which attends our every waking moment. In case his dire warnings about World Cup frenzy might be construed as sour grapes (no way!) he also lashed the Rose of Tralee as an orgy of drink. He might as well be trying to drain the Corrib with a straw.

LOGAN, Johnny

Winning the Eurovision once might be deemed unfortunate. Winning it twice is just carelessness. Three times, and you'd better quit while you're behind. Conspiracy theorists advanced the view that Johnny was involved in a plot to bankrupt RTE, but in fact they love Eurovision out in Montrose, because it gives them an excuse not to spend money on proper programmes. Johnny is big in places like Turkey, and taunts the critics by inviting them to look at the size of his car. He has done his bit. But for what?
See Harrington, Paul.

LOVE, Clayton

The only Cork merchant prince with a name redolent of black exploitation movies.
See Barry, Peter.

LOWE, Teresa

Presenter of *Where In The World*, she gives good quiz. It is widely known that she is married to Frank MacNamara, who gives good ivory. "I wonder who wears the trousers in that house?" Perhaps neither of them do. Teresa proved that she has brains as well as beauty by passing her Bar exams, securing a higher

mark than the mature student, Vincent Browne. Perhaps she would like to edit the *Sunday Tribune*. Everything seems possible for her and her lovely husband.

LUCEY, Dr. Mary

It would be wrong to think that Dr. Lucey is solely concerned with abortion. She is also against contraception, divorce and homosexuality, and is one of those people who go on the radio to complain about not being on the radio.

LUNNY, Donal

Even more multi-talented than Teresa Lowe, and ahead on points over Frank MacNamara, Donal extracted the poker from the ass of traditional music, and made it groove to the rhythms of the world. The bouzouki used to remind us of Nana Mouskouri. Now it reminds us of Planxty and Moving Hearts and all of that mighty sound engineered by the man they call Donal Lunny. For that is his name.

LYNAM, Ray

A freak of nature, the genial Moateman somehow got it into his head that an Irish person could play country'n'western without making a total eejit out of himself. Many have followed the path of quality, but Ray was the first. Let us salute him.

LYNCH, Danny (no relation)

In The "Dear John" letters, he was anxious to dispel any suspicion that he and your correspondent are the same person, or in any way related. He agreed that many people in his organisation would like my citizenship to be revoked, but thought that it would only give me the notoriety that I crave. One must understand that being PRO of the GAA has its pressures. Danny Lynch is only human. Or something.

LYNCH, Jack

He represents the era when a proficiency in Gaelic Games automatically entitled you to run the country, if you so pleased. Apparently devoid of personal ambition, Gentleman Jack secured a massive majority for Fianna Fáil, and then it all went horribly, horribly wrong. Since he retired, the pipe has largely gone out of politics.

LYNCH, Joe

Dinny from *Glenroe*. He once played Elsie Tanner's taxi-driving boyfriend in *Coronation Street,* and is possessed of a fine singing voice. Sued a newspaper. Say no more.

MAC, Joe

Madcap drummer and all round exhibitionist with The Dixies, he was one zany guy. A sign outside the Southern capital says, "Welcome

To Cork, Home Of The Dixies." Paris is the home of the Louvre, Rome is the home of the Forum, and Cork is the home of The Dixies. Every city is unique unto itself.

MacARTHUR, Malcolm

The bow-tied degenerate gave new meaning to the term "hammer man", and a new word to the language, GUBU, when he rested up in the apartment of the Attorney-General – one Patrick Connolly at the time – after his murderous exertions in the Phoenix Park. John Banville is thought to have based the novel *The Book Of Evidence* on this person, a bit of a change from Newton, Kepler and Copernicus. In Arbour Hill, he has acquired computer skills.

See Whelehan, Harry.

MacGIOLLA, Tomás

He used to demonstrate washing-machines in people's homes, and reckons that he did the washing for half of Dublin. He later tried to sell encyclopedias to the other half. He's had a few embarrassing jobs as well, fighting for the IRA, slogging for the Workers Party, and being Lord Mayor of Dublin. It's been a full life for Tom Gill.

MacMATHUNA, Ciarán

His Master's Voice is redolent of a time when music presenters were expected to conduct themselves with dignity. Before the "Beat On The Street", instead of prancing around a stage like a Kansas City faggot, Ciaran would visit the parlours of Ireland, recording tunes for posterity. He is married to the lovely Dolly. Hello Dolly.

MacTHOMÁIS, Eamonn

"Ah me jewel and darlin' Dublin sure poor oul' Jemmy Joyce and poor oul' Deano Swift up there in the Cathedral didn't know the half of it, queuin' outside the Maro with a package of bullseyes and an oringe I'll tell you Brian Boru was the only man who could beat them Danes." Ah blow it out your ass.

MacRÉAMOINN, Seán

In an interview, he said that he was like a Census Form — broken down by age, sex and religion. His many contributions to the discovery of the Irish mind are respected, but I think that this one will outlive us all. It's been a full life for John Redmond.

McALEER, Kevin

Due to an extraordinary error, McAleer's dead-pan portrayals of mad country people came to prominence on RTE's *Nighthawks.* The error was quickly spotted, and the show taken off the air.

See Hughes, Sean.

McBRIDE, Tom
See Tom, Big.

McBRIDE, Willie John
He took even fewer prisoners than Moss Keane. Geneva Convention? Never heard of it. While performing mighty deeds in the green shirt, he was also a Bank Manager. "Now, about that overdraft you owe me" . . .
See Keane, Moss.

McCABE, Patrick
His wonderful novel *The Butcher Boy* has a trailer which reads thus: "Patrick McCabe has written a mesmeric tale of horror and pathos, and created a jagged world of scorn and fear, of turned backs and unspoken insults, a world to which it is impossible to belong unless you know the rules of the game." He knows his Monaghan.

McCAFFERTY, Nell
She introduced poor people to the *Irish Times* with her Court reports. Soon they were everywhere. Poor people and women too. Poor women, even. Nell has done more for poor women than Mother Teresa, in that she didn't see much percentage in them remaining poor and having loads of children to keep God in a good mood. Probably the first woman to smoke on RTE television, she is one of that special breed of Irish people instantly recognised by their first name. There's Daniel and Gay and Garret and Charlie and Jack and Christy, there's Bono,

Adam, Larry and Edge . . . they all come under the thunder of Nell.

McCANN, Donal

Thanks to his many television and movie roles, the general public does not have to go to the theatre to savour the McCann experience. Not that they would, anyway. They can also hear his voice advertising anything from mineral water to cream to Fianna Fáil. Critics believe that his greatest role was in Brian Friel's *Faith Healer*. Time to get that on video and let the people decide.

McCANN, Eamonn

Alphabetically, geographically, and politically adjacent to Nell, he is instantly recognised by his second name. "Did you see your man McCann?" is as explanatory as "did you see your man Dunphy?" They don't make such men in job lots. There are senior Vatican officials who do not know as much about the appalling history of Catholicism as McCann, and wouldn't admit it if they did. When a bishop denounced moving statues, he wrote: "Here is a man who, on a daily basis, purports to transform quantities of bread and wine into the body and blood of a person who allegedly lived 2,000 years ago. I think he has a cheek." A compulsive orator, he has been pictured holding the Sam Maguire Cup.

McCAUGHRAN, Tom

RTE's Security Correspondent is also the author of best-selling novels about animals. From Garda headquarters to the great outdoors, he is drawn by the call of the wild.

McCREEVY, Charlie

The former maverick has agonised about the direction of Fianna Fáil, as though it had a direction, other than cosying up to the nearest trough. Everything usually turns out for the best, the trough is emptied, and Ireland remains free. On "social issues" (sex and stuff) Charlie would be on the liberal wing of the Party. That's quite close to being normal, but no cigar.

McCULLAGH, Wayne

The Pocket Rocket looks set for a shot at The Title. After his Olympic bid, he must have formed the impression that success means being brought to Gaelic matches and introduced to the crowd. Wee Wayne survived that too, and it only remains to be seen whether he can go the whole way and become the next Barry McGuigan. Then the craic will start in earnest.

McDAID, James

On the "liberal" wing of Fianna Fáil, he is one of an elite group in the history of Irish politics who has actually resigned over something, albeit with a lot of help from Dessie O'Malley. It was felt that a Minister for Defence ought not to have been photographed in the vicinity of rabid Republicans. He was later rejected in his bid to join the Women's Group in Leinster House, on the grounds that he is not, and has no intention of becoming, a woman.

McDONALD, Frank

Whenever there are brown paper bags being passed around, you will find Frank, scourge of the cowboy "developer" and the crooked councillor. His writings rail against the building of poxy bungalows in areas of outstanding natural beauty. He was one of the first people to realise that Ireland has an environment. Or should that be had?

McDOWELLS, The

Though they masquerade as a Progressive Democrat, an economist, and a Labour TD, it is thought that they are the same person, who haunts the corridors of RTE, appearing on radio and television as often as decency will permit. With the addition of a false beard, Michael becomes Moore, and with a subtle make-up job, it's Derek the socialist. The three-in-one trick is borrowed from God, who receives far less air-time nowadays than The McDowells.

McENTEE, Patrick

The greatest defence lawyer in the world. If you bludgeon six people to death with a lump hammer on live, prime time television, shouting "I'm glad I killed the bastards," just ask for Paddy and you'll march out of that courthouse a free man, screaming that there's no justice, and that you'll have to wait ten fornicating years for compensation. Some people may be just too monstrously guilty even for Paddy's talents. But not many.

McGAHERN, John

The artist has made Leitrim his home, perhaps for the eerie quietude which reigns in its de-peopled land. It is probably the only place where he can step out of his door without someone inviting him to a black-tie dinner to accept an award. Either he starts writing bad books, or spends the rest of his life eating big dinners and collecting trophies.

McGAHON, Brendan

On *Questions & Answers,* the Louth-mouth addressed a member of the audience thus: "If you prefer to go to bed with a man rather than a woman, I feel sorry for you, *a mhic.*" When speaking his mind, he tells you that he is speaking his mind. His mind is of the view that rapists should be castrated, but humanely, like they do in Mississippi. Flogging and hanging also meet with his approval, but he believes that Coursing is barbaric. I'd take that seriously if I were a Courser.

McGOLDRICK, Anna

"Let him go, let him tarry, let him sink or let him swim, he doesn't care for me, and I don't care for him. Let him go and find another one, I hope he will enjoy. But I'd rather marry a far nicer boy." One can never hear these words without thinking of Anna McGoldrick. She made a record number of appearances on *Opportunity Knocks* when these things mattered.

McGOWAN, Shane

"He is so talented. Why does he drink so

much?" I don't know. Perhaps he likes drinking. He doesn't drink as much as he used to, but he enjoys a glass of wine with a meal.

McGRATH, Paul

Ireland's best and best-loved footballer, he is a poet who has desisted from writing goddamn poetry. Tabloid frenzy about his private life has added "a bad knee" to popular lore, signifying an excess of alcohol. On being awarded the Freedom of Dublin, Nelson Mandela was honoured with the chant, "ooh, aah, Paul McGrath's da." To unwind, Paul likes to go missing in County Cork.

McGUIGAN, Barry

It appeared to surprise some people that the Clones Cyclone's heroic career ended in the ignominy of legal wranglings and lost opportunities. For boxers, this is as commonplace as the gold watch on retirement, virtually a cliche. Sayings include "thank you very much, Mr. Eastwood" – and a lot of other things about Mr. Eastwood which didn't stand up in court.

McGUINNESS, Frank

A new McGuinness is always an occasion of excitement on the theatrical front, where the regulars are joined by a few curious members of the general public. The old McGuinnesses are still paying their way too. Frank is a dab hand at the Old Norse, but hell, who cares? Good plays, good guy.

McGUINNESS, Martin

He may refute the allegation that he is Boss man of the IRA or indeed that he ever *was* Boss Man of the IRA but he cannot deny his birthright as a concerned Catholic, and devoted family man. Martin takes time out from his onerous commitments in the contemplative setting of the river-bank, where he indulges his enthusiasm for angling. We know so little of the private man behind the public face. One looks forward to learning more about Martin McGuinness, angler extraordinaire, in the colour supplements.

McGUINNESS, Paul

Without the services of their taciturn manager, it is arguable that U2 might still be wowing them at the El Ruedo in Carlow, or Sligo's Blue Lagoon. Having been sent down from Trinity College for describing someone as "a cunt", it was clear that rock'n'roll would provide an outlet for his talents. Paul was no doubt alarmed when his line "I only had to be right once" was later echoed in a crude form by the Provisional IRA describing their 'mainland' bombing campaign. He has assisted the Simon Community.

McINTYRE, Tom

For a former Cavan footballer, he writes extraordinarily difficult plays. It is indeed rare for

97

avant-garde dramatists to emerge from the ranks of the GAA, but McIntyre broke the mould. The punters may come around eventually, but it's a slow old slog.

McKENNA, Barney

A legend among legends, the ace banjo-picker is especially legendary for approaching Ted Kennedy in O'Donoghues and saying "sorry about the brothers." In the company of your correspondent, he drank white wine out of a pint glass because he was not in the form for a real drink. He has communed with a Native American tribe.

McKEON, Clare

The only thing standing in the way of her becoming Ireland's Oprah Winfrey is that there are not as many twisted fuckers in Ireland as there are in America, dying to share their problems with the masses. But are there enough? Clare must make do with *Suite Talk* for now, sharing a platform with Cynthia Ní Mhurchú, and grilling people who wish to be considered sane. They are out there, Clare, and no better woman to reel them in.
See Ní Mhurchú, Cynthia.

McLOUGHLIN, Alan

He silenced the bear-pit of Windsor Park with his buccaneering equaliser, and was then completely ignored by Big Jack during the World Cup. "Just get me a goal," Jack had said. Little did Alan realise that nothing was required of him thereafter.

McMANUS, J.P.
High roller extraordinaire, he is to be found wherever men speculate to accumulate, be it Cheltenham, Vegas or the Telecom site in Ballsbridge. Racehorse owner, bookmaker, and warrior punter, he has accumulated enough to live in Switzerland, where he might hold on to it in peace.

McNAMARA, Angela
For years, she dispensed motherly advice in the *Sunday Press* about the perils of sex before marriage, and the problems of sex after marriage to boot. She was widely read and her wisdom duly noted. God bless us all.

McNEILL, Hugo
The lovely Hugo is a near-perfect human being, an International rugby star, an intellectual powerhouse, a thespian, and a really good bloke, you know? Unlike Willie John or Moss, he took prisoners, and allowed them a bit of a ramble in the exercise yard. He is over in London now, making money. Hopefully.

McSHARRY, Ray
His formative experiences as a Sligo cattle-dealer were the perfect preparation for life at the cutting edge of macro-economics. International travel has altered his accent somewhat, but not the jet-black sheen of his

hair. He suffered anti-Irish abuse at the pen of Robert Kilroy-Silk, even though he doesn't drink. Jacques Delors queried his expenses.

McVERRY, Fr. Peter

Clongowes-educated, he seems to have completely misunderstood his Jesuit instructors. They didn't really *mean* that the rich would help the poor, they just wanted them to feel bad about it now and again. His work with homeless boys is widely praised, but he is something of an outcast himself, as he is totally disinterested in his Church's campaigns against human sexuality. For McVerry, rubber johnnies are not the main event.

MAGEE, Jimmy

Compiler of Ireland's first Top 20, Jimmy is firmly on the showband wing of sport, where his All-Stars selections have raised money for charity and cemented friendships throughout the chicken-in-a-basket circuit. Before the computer data-base, Jimmy's mind contained the world's most comprehensive stock of arcane information about any subject. He is literally a know-all. His awesome powers of recall will remind him of the time that he had Platini playing inside Brady's shorts for 45 minutes, and of "the symbol of peace — the pigeon!"

MAGINNIS, Ken

Derided by hardline loyalists as a Free State lackey, Ken is the only leading Unionist who bears a passing resemblance to a member of the Village People.

MALOCCA, Elio

The celebrity solicitor had high-profile clients such as Fr. Paddy Ryan, until eventually his own profile took centre stage, and he was required to defend himself, inter alia, against the De Valera family and the Twink family over the whereabouts of certain monies. So he went to New York to carve out a career in the film industry, as you would. When he returned to Dublin, he worked in a restaurant.
See Ryan, Fr. Paddy.

MALONE, Bernie

Battling Bernie defied the Party big-shots and the more telegenic, photogenic, possibly even antiseptic Orla Guerin to become an MEP. The electorate wished her well in Strasbourg. "Bye bye, don't forget us," they said.

MALLON, Seamus

Unlike his Party leader, Mallon occasionally leaves the television studio to spend some time in Betting Offices, his home away from home. "He is a man the Unionists could do business with," they say. Only if they take out a bookmaker's licence, sez you.
See Hume, John.

MANNING, Maurice

From the bunkers of UCD to the fairways of Leinster House he has chipped away, losing the odd ball in the process. His book on The Blueshirts is the definitive work on that fine body of men. Everything you ever wanted to know about Eoin O'Duffy in one concise volume. "I laughed out loud."

101

MANSERGH, Martin

A mandarin, he can be seen hovering in the background when our loodheramawn elected representatives are signing Treaties. He has done the thinking for men too busy to do it themselves, placing a gloss of literacy on their primitive ramblings. The poshest Republican in town, he is rarely photographed. It helps that in the Gershwin term, he is unphotographable. It's the glasses, Martin.

MARA, P. J.

Unlike Mansergh, Mara represented the views of Charles J.Haughey with boundless conviviality. At one of his press briefings, known as "the five o'clock follies", he made what he thought were humourous remarks about people biting his leader's bum, and the policy of *una duce, una voce.* More sombre souls were soon writing long articles citing this as prime evidence of the megalomania of Mara's boss. Boulevardier and raconteur, his genius lay in telling journalists wonderful stories about the appalling personal perversions of politicians, stories which were true but totally unprintable. His witticisms are renowned, not least the one describing Fr. Paddy Ryan as a member of the Pallottine Liberation Organisation. A "Charlie Man" with knobs on.
See Haughey, Charles J.

MARSHALL, David

Ireland's answer to Vidal Sassoon, he coiffed his way to a fortune by identifying a gap in the market for funny haircuts. His staff were experimenting with people's heads at a time when we had just become accustomed to shampoo as a non-luxury product. He has been seen drinking with Alex Higgins.

MARTIN, Linda
Eurovision winner, Eurovision runner-up, she has a wealth of experience at all levels of Irish showbusiness. Perhaps it is no coincidence that she chooses to spend most of her spare time with quadrupeds.

MATHEWS, Philip
Zoologist and captain of the Irish rugby team, few men have so seamlessly combined business with pleasure. He took more prisoners than Moss Keane or Willie John McBride, but a few of them just escaped.
See Keane, Moss; McBride, Willie John.

MERCIER, Paul
A lion of the theatre, he has achieved the near-impossible by persuading members of the general public to attend his plays. This has made him something of an outcast from the establishment, who go to great lengths to ensure that the general public would prefer to watch Cliff Richard at The Point.

MILLS, Michael
The Ombudsman, just retired. Dial his successor at 6785222.

MITCHELL, Gay
He goes rigid at the sight of a microphone, expounding Fine Gael policy to beat the band. He is particularly tough on crime, agreeing with

103

the electorate that it is a bad thing, and that there should be less of it. His own contribution to human misery is the political quiz-book, a genre in which he almost the sole practitioner, for obvious reasons. Wants to bring the Olympics to Dublin.

MITCHELL, Jim

Affectionately dubbed The Fixer, he is often described as a working-class boy made good. The working-class have mixed views about this. With brother Gay, he shares a family trait of becoming aroused at the sight of a microphone. From certain angles, he can look like he is wearing a false nose, even though he is not. Probably. He looks much younger without his specs.

MOLLOY, Bobby

The ageless Íosagáin joined the Fianna Fáil mutiny which led to the formation of the PDs. He was not a "Charlie Man". More of a "Bobby Man" perhaps. He has occasionally been mistaken for Vincent Browne, a matter of no great amusement to either of them. He has a great future behind him.

MOLONEY, Paddy

The Chieftains' chieftain, uileann pipes notwithstanding, is a hell of a nice fella. He has been invited to play with numerous legends of rock, and will invariably tell you that Paul McCartney, Jackson Browne and Ricky Scaggs are all one hell of a nice fellow. Van Morrison? A hell of a nice fella. He also manages the financial affairs of The Chieftains (Paddy, not Van), clearly unable to find a fella nice enough in this area of the business. "He is a great ambassador," they say, combining jigs and reels with international diplomacy. Sayings include "round the house" and "mind the dresser."

MOONEY, Paschal

No man has done more to further the cause of Country'n'Irish music than Rambo from Drumshanbo, the disc-jockey and Senator. A spiritual kinsman to Senator Donie Cassidy, he

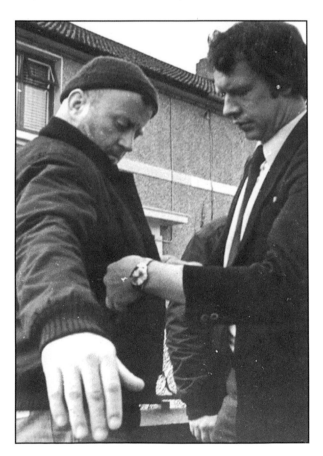

is strong on "family values" and the traditional ethos which has served his native county so well that the majority of its people now live on a different Continent. Carlene Carter wanted to "put the cunt back into Country." Paschal would prefer to leave it be.

See Cassidy, Donie.

MOORE, Christy

Hailed as the Greatest Living Irishman by Shane McGowan, Christy has shown that you can be great, living, and Irish without being a sanctimonious, God-bothering,

105

unctuous, fáinne-wearing, simpering clown. Along with Foster & Allen, he is one of those artistes whose records are bought by people who don't buy records. As distinct from Foster & Allen, Christy's records have music on them. He has had a racehorse named after him.

MORAN, Kevin

The Greatest Living Irishman in Short Trousers, there are those who would seek to tarnish Kevin's reputation by dragging him into politics. He has resisted the urge, preferring to emulate Hector Grey as a gift-shop magnate. Because Kevin is the most blindingly obvious person to succeed Jack Charlton, he can be considered eliminated from the contest. "He puts his head where others would be afraid to put their boots."

MORGAN, Dermot

The satirical *Scrap Saturday* was such an enormous popular hit, RTE had to move with great determination to yank it off the air. There is a certain inevitability about the proposition that the richly talented Morgan will become an international comedy star, and then someone will ask an RTE executive, "what do you think of that?" "We are very pleased for Dermot, and are happy to be associated with his early career," the exec. will say. Then he will be shot.

MORRISSEY, Louise

On the Louise Morrissey video, *Memories Of Home,* the tracks 'Amazing Grace', 'Slievenamon' and 'The Old Rustic Bridge' are partially credited to Senator Donie Cassidy, even though he is known not to have written them. Presumably, he just improved them.

MORRISON, Van

There have been moves afoot in the journalistic community to form a secret society of people who have interviewed Van Morrison. They will meet every year to compare their experiences and share the pain. Van may have a problem with the old sound-bytes, but that album he's been putting out for the last fifteen years still sounds sublime. And it's too late to

stop now. In his autumn years, he has alarmed the fans of *T.B.Sheets* by hanging out with Cliff Richard, Richard Gere, and various other Dicks in the stately homes of Ireland. His stage show has accommodated the diverse talents of Paul Durcan and Michelle Rocca. For a man raised by Jehovah's Witnesses in the wilds of Belfast, he has opened many doors.
See Durcan, Paul; Rocca, Michelle.

MOUNTCHARLES, Henry

More people have had more fun in Mounty's back garden than they ever dreamed possible. But somewhere along the way, an unseen enemy began to stick needles in a voodoo doll called Henry Mountcharles — something to do with Fine Gael, perhaps? First, the castle burnt down, and then he got caught in the Lloyd's fiasco, hilarious to the common man, no joke for Mounty at all. He has borne his hardships with some style, though it may be time to change those lucky odd socks.

MULCAHY, Mick

The eccentric painter travels to places like Papua New Guinea to seek inspiration for his art, and to find himself. A free spirit, he enjoys dancing barefoot in nite-clubs. Got married and then unmarried with remarkable alacrity. He bears a remarkable resemblance to the cowboy on the Dublin Bus ads for Bad Bob's honky-tonk.

MULLEN Jnr., Larry

The shop steward of U2, Larry would have been good-looking even without wealth and

fame. No Ringo Starr he. A good-living man, he has a passion for motorbikes which gives manager Paul McGuinness the odd tremor. Larry is the only musician to have played electric and acoustic sets at Croke Park, with U2 and the Artane Boys Band respectively. Boy George is in love with him.

MULVIHILL, Liam

General Secretary of the GAA, it has fallen to him on occasion to lead the chorus of good wishes to Jack Charlton's boys during the World Cup. He does his best, but it still looks like one of those video-tapes of hostages saying that they're fine, they're fine, and would someone please pay the ransom.

See Boothman, Jack ; Lynch, Danny.

MURPHY, Arthur

His *Mailbag* programme was an invaluable platform for the ridiculous opinions of telly-addicts and assorted headbangers. He would try to make the show "madder" by wearing funny hats, which was gilding the lily some-what. A bit of a "character".

MURPHY, Christina

Headmistress of the *Irish Times* Department of Education. 20,000 words on the Geography syllabus and she's only warming up. A martyr to learning. A saint.

MURPHY, Mike

Ireland's answer to Terry Wogan, he applies a light touch to the worlds of business, finance, the law, and the Arts. If there is a thread run-ning through his multi-purpose career, it is money. Mike has given away a shocking amount of other people's money on *Winning Streak* and *Up And Running* and a plethora of game shows. Mr. Affability gives the impres-sion of having retired, even though he is on television and radio all the time. People see him constantly on TV, and wonder, "whatever happened to him?" It's all in the mind.

MURPHY, Tom

There is a school of thought that Theatre can't be a complete load of bollocks if Tom Murphy is involved in it. His chosen genre has deprived the community at large of his genius, but he carries on, the wounded lion. A lover of opera and wine, he once poured a pint of beer over the head of a newspaper editor. "I don't like you," he explained. He also had to explain to critics that it was not valid to fault a work of art because it prevented punters getting the last bus home. Murphy is big enough to admit an antipathy to Beckett. Crazy plays, crazy guy.

MYERS, Kevin

Humourist, War Correspondent, Quizmaster, and Professor of Satire at the *Irish Times,* Myers is at his most brilliant when writing about bugger-all. As we luxuriate in the plushness of his prose, we eventually discover that there is some cryptic pretext. A meditation on the Great War will finally reveal that a Frenchman has signed for Shamrock Rovers. And France fought in the Great War. Obvious, isn't it? In Republican circles, he is seen as the most Westerly of all the West Brits. "Kevin Myarse," they jeer. He is above all that.

NEESON, Liam

Thousands of articles have been written about Liam's affairs with "a string of beautiful women." In fact it is the same article written thousands of times, in which we learn that Liam prefers the company of women, that he is very gentle for a big man, and that the collective name for beautiful women is "a string". There is much innuendo suggesting that he possesses an exceptionally large penis. His acting career is going great guns as well.

NEWMAN, Bishop

Jeremiah of Limerick is on the conservative wing of the hierarchy, slightly to the right of

trendier bishops who only favour the doctrinal cat-of-eight-tails. Unlike them, his name has never been associated with a string of beautiful women. Very learned. Likes a drop.
See Casey, Bishop.

NÍ MHURCHÚ, Cynthia

She's got it all, in both national languages. It will be interesting to see how RTE contrives to make the least of her talents over the coming years, but giving her the Eurovision was an interesting start. Like Teresa Lowe, she has taken out insurance against an uncertain future by studying for the Bar. It helps to know your rights. Is she ambitious? Yes and no. Yes, she is ambitious, and no, she is very ambitious.

NOLAN, Finbarr

The seventh son of a seventh son, and perhaps even the seventh son of a seventh son of a seventh son, and so on into infinity, he became a celebrity healer. When Uri Geller was bending forks, Finbarr was curing ringworm and rheumatism and making new strides in alternative medicine generally. *Sunday World* reporters were often present to witness his miracles, and take photographs. "He is driven away in a limousine after making the blind see and the poor prosper." Where is he now?

NOONAN, Michael

There are two Michael Noonans. The bald one is renowned for his acid wit in the Fine Gael interest. The one they call "Cowshed" has no reputation for any kind of wit, but can be heard espousing the core values of Fianna Fáil, whatever the fuck they may be, and slamming the "liberal agenda". Michael Noonan and Michael Noonan. Limerick must choose.

NORRIS, David

Of the PDs, he said that they alienated 80% of the people by taking God out of the Constitution, and alienated the other 20% by putting Him back in. Of Archbishop Connell, he said that the man may know a lot about angels, but he knows nothing about fairies. The terminally Joycean Senator has joked about being Ireland's only homosexual. Famous for renovating his house, he is under the impression that he lives in Dublin's Inner City.

See Hanly, David; Connell, Archbishop; Shine, Brendan.

Ó'BRÁDAIGH, Ruairí

A relic of a vanished civilisation. God bless us and save us.

O'BRIEN

He had nowhere to go.
See Shine, Brendan.

O'BRIEN, Conor Cruise

If David Norris was Ireland's first homosexual, The Cruiser was our first atheist, then our first agnostic, and possibly our first intellectual. His crusade against the original "Charlie Man" has entertained him for decades. It was such fruitful territory that it produced a new word,

GUBU. The Provisional IRA brings out the Cassandra in him. They will do this, that, and the other, cue mushroom cloud, Armageddon, End of World. Outside of the more secure mental health establishments, he was among the few who thought that Internment was a good idea. Having infuriated just about every segment of society over the years, it is fair to say that he is probably the most hated man in Ireland.

O'BRIEN, Edna

One of Ireland's most beautiful women, she did a bit of acid in her day. And why not? Her already teeming imagination had yielded up a flock of country girls coming to terms with their sexuality in this crazy little country we call "home". Celebrated for her intense womanliness, and her mama-will-make-it-better voice, she has been photographed with Gerry Adams, united in literature, a lovely couple altogether. Does Gerry write his own stuff too? Mama will make it better.

O'BRIEN, Mick

He was Athlone Town's goalkeeper for the Nineties. This was during the Seventies. I can still hear the crash of that crossbar that he broke during the FAI Cup semi-final against Finn Harps, and see his dashes up the green sward to assist the midfield. You can see the likes of Peter Schmeichel doing this sort of thing now, but it is a jaded travesty of this great innovator. "Is there a carpenter in the ground?"

O'BYRNE, Arnold

The Opel super-salesman sounds like he needs a refund from that voice-coach. In four small words – put the boot in – he takes us into uncharted territory of metre and emphasis and pronunciation. His sentences conduct a war within themselves, fighting for alien territory, which may explain why he struck up such a relationship with Big Jack. They speak the same language.
See Charlton, Jack ; Kilcoyne, Louis.

O'BYRNES, Stephen

The anti-charismatic PD press officer ran for "Europe" on the slogan "Simply The Best". This was policy as formulated by Tina Turner, and Stephen's head didn't quite fit the message. It was like Norman Wisdom touting himself as "mean, moody, magnificent". He got slaughtered.

O'CARROLL, Brendan

We expected him to be RTE's World Cup trump card, talking to the Green Army about the state of their mickeys, the size of their moustaches (or his), and the problems of getting ratarsed in a strange land. Instead he finished up wandering around Orlando with Niall Quinn, asking people what part they were from, and being friendly to policemen. At home, he is brilliant at relating the humour of vicious old Dublin women and their barabaric worldview. "The women love him."

O'CLERY, Conor

He now holds the Chair of American Studies at the *Irish Times*, having paid his dues as head of the Russian Department and Dean of the Faculty of Northern Ireland. He was one of those smart Catholics who emerged from The North after decades of apartheid. He survived all this to remain a first-rate reporter.

O'CONNELL, Mick

The greatest Gaelic player of all time, he graced the era when GAA players didn't speak in public, some even less than others. Legends grew to fill the primeval silence, like how Micko forgot to bring home the Sam Maguire Cup because he had urgent business on Valentia. He was the last man to travel to a training session in a rowing-boat.

O'CONNOR, Pat,

A "Charlie Man" to the core, he was christened Pat O'Connor, but became better known as Pat O'Connor, Pat O'Connor when, as election agent for "Charlie", he faced accusations of voting twice. He was a divil for democracy.

O'CONNOR, Sinéad

Tearing up pictures of The Pope and denigrating the American National Anthem were once considered to be desirable, nay mandatory inclinations in a rock'n'roller. Now, withered old degenerates gather to praise Bob Dylan and to heckle Sinéad for such trifles. And they think that she is the sad one, the bastards. The only hint that she may be going the way of all California herself was a dedication to her psychiatrist on the last album. But it was Dr. Anthony Clare, who is on the showbusiness wing. This decent woman is dealing with her problems. For scores of Irish entertainers there was no Tony Clare, and it's too late now.

O'CONNOR, Ulick

One of our livelier men of letters, he strove for the Corinthian ideal, *mens sano in corpore sano* and all that jazz. After Ulick you found fewer writers who were proficient in high-jumping and boxing. It is hard to imagine John Banville and Paul Durcan stepping outside and putting up their dukes in the manner of Ulick and Brendan Behan. Then there is his enthusiasm for Noh plays, whatever the jaysus they may be. A writer like Roddy Doyle is more of a man for the Noh Fucking Way Pal genre. None of the "Abbey Style" there, but plenty of bums on seats. Come out Ulick, and show them who's boss.

O'CONOR, John

The great ivory-tickler has tried to cajole us into the ways of high-class culture by telling us that classical music can be great fun once you get the hang of it. We are just happy that he has got the hang of it, and leave well enough alone. Play on, John O'Conor, play on.

O'DEA, Willie

An expert in Law and Taxation, it naturally fell to the feisty deputy from Bruff to tackle Dublin's heroin problem. While pondering the mysteries of smack, he found time to castigate the legal profession for their ridiculous court-room attire. In The Dáil, Pat Rabbitte TD called him "the Danny De Vito of Fianna Fáil", but no-one knows what he meant by this.

O'DONNELL, Daniel

His amazing magnetism draws women from Australia to share a cuppa in his front garden with women of like mind. Not so much a singer as a way of life, Daniel is the nice young curate who will listen to your problems without expecting you to get your kit off for a six-in-the-bed romp. In his ripping *Sunday World* column, he has "written" of the war in former Yugoslavia. He is against it.

O'DOWDA, Brendan

In more innocent times, this popular singer appeared on an album cover with a sheep. This was a period of Irish graphic design when musicians were often pictured in agricultural settings. Nowadays, questions would be raised.

Ó'DÚLAING, Donncha

Dublin Four was probably invented to counter-act the extraordinary view of old Ireland gleaned by Donncha from his lengthy conversations with oul' fellas and oul' wans and Brother this and Canon that, and all that mighty residue of a vanished civilisation. Having established the Munster Final as the crucible of Western culture, he embarked on a series of pilgrimages, walking vast distances to places of religious and historical interest. No-one shouted stop.

O'FAOLAIN, Nuala

Of her many outstanding *Irish Times* columns, perhaps the most notable was one in which she defended me against charges of blasphemy levelled by Bishop Brendan Comiskey and his sad friends. There is a great need for more journalism of this calibre. The wisdom and wit of her writings is matched only by the warmth and charm of her TV presentations. She is a fine person.

O'GORMAN, Paddy

The award-winning reporter chronicles the lifestyles of the poor and unknown at their places of unemployment. He is a sort of Terry Keane for people who make less than fifty quid a week. His indefatigable pursuit of the marginalised is entirely laudible, though if you see him approaching, microphone cocked, you are probably worse off than you think.

O'HANLON, Ardal

A remarkable and little-known fact about this brilliant young comedian is that he is the son of Dr. Rory O'Hanlon, big in Fianna Fáil. It is surprisingly common for the scions of

Government Ministers to become professional stand-up comedians. Usually, however, they describe themselves as politicians or auctioneers. Ardal has broken the mould.

O'HANLON, Judge Rory

High Court judge and father-of-twelve, he is also a fertile source of controversy, due to his membership of the Opus Dei cult, in which guise he issues statements condemning the moral atrophy which he perceives all around him. Critics argue about whether Opus Dei is a hobby or a full-time job. This is a dangerous

argument, as it would question the right of, say, Hare Krishnas to ascend to senior judicial posts. The bench is conspicuously short of Hare Krishnas, and this must change.

O'HARA, Mary

She embodied a certain vision of Irish womanhood, chaste, plucking at a harp, available for

weddings and funerals. Hovering in an ethereal space between this world of woes and the sanctuary of the convent. And clean. Always clean. She was Enya without attitude.
See Enya.

O'HERLIHY, Bill

He has the most important job in the country, monitoring the public pulse as Jack's Army goes into the fray. A stupid jacket, a badly-aimed jibe, or a simple error of mood, and the Moderator of the RTE panel is dead meat. Still on top of the case, he has a successful PR company, and he helped Garret FitzGerald to become Taoiseach. But that's just a bit of sport.

O'HIGGINS, Tom

He nearly became President of Ireland instead of De Valera, and had to console himself with all manner of big jobs in the judging trade. How different would things have been if the Fine Gael man had prevailed over the Long Fellow? Hmmm, it's a teaser.

O'KEEFFE, Batt

Another of those "colourful" Cork deputies, he upholds the tradition of Leeside politicians with funny names. There's Batt, and Dino, and Dano, and Bosey, and Dimples, but no Snow White as yet. We await the emergence of the next generation, Dave Dee, Dozy, Beaky, Mick and Titch.

O'KEEFFE, Ned

After an exhausting but exhilarating day at the

Spring Show, the colourful Fianna Fáil deputy made unwelcome overtures to RTE's political correspondent Una Claffey in the Dáil Bar. Charles Haughey admonished him for this. It must have been quite an occasion for both of them. He subsequently castigated the environmental lobby for "shouting and roaring like a pack of Balubas," courageously jeopardising that important Central African vote. A bit of a "character".

O'KEEFFE, Susan

In keeping with the incredible logic of the Beef Tribunal Report, it was only natural that the one person to face criminal charges was the journalist who kick-started it. People thought that this made no sense. On the contrary, it made perfect sense.

See Hamilton, Judge.

O'KELLY, Fachtna

His was the first voice on RTE radio describing Country'n'Irish records as the horse-shit that they were. Eventually he went on to manage the Boomtown Rats, Bananarama and Sinéad O'Connor, all of which made him exceedingly thin. He is thought to be one of the few Irish pop managers with a functioning brain.

O'LEARY, David

Spurned by Big Jack for all the wrong reasons, Gentleman Dave kept his dignity and secured a place among the immortals by wrapping up the penalty shoot-out against Rumania in Italia '90. Mercifully, it was only afterwards we learned that the last penalty Dave took in

123

anger was when he was a small boy.

O'LEARY, Olivia

It's Thursday, it's *Prime Time,* and it's bollocks. Olivia did her best, but after too many nights inclining her head at a difficult angle in the direction of tedious Government functionaries, she jumped RTE's Current Affairs flagship. In happier times, during the Falklands War, she foiled the Argie censors by filing her copy *as Gaeilge*. The Irish Department of the *Irish Times* translated it, and a stroke had been pulled which would give a 'Charlie Man' a raging 24-hour erection which would open up a furrow on the Long Acre. One of the greats, her print journalism is flawed by the occasional use of the words "dinner" and "party".

O'MAHONY, Andy

There are at leat two Andy O'Mahonys — the cheerful fellow who shoots the breeze with all-comers on *The Sunday Show*, and the cerebral person who talks to very brainy people on programmes with names like "Digressions", "Soundings", "Tangents", "Dialogue", and "Lamp Post". He is smaller in real life than his voice suggests.

O'MALLEY, Des

He was as sick as an aviary full of diseased parrots as his golden boy Pat Cox shafted him and his Party in the Euro elections. To the "Charlie Man", he is Lucifer living in Limerick, and the pleasure they take in his political demise surpasses the mere sexual. This was even better than cutting his throat and throw-

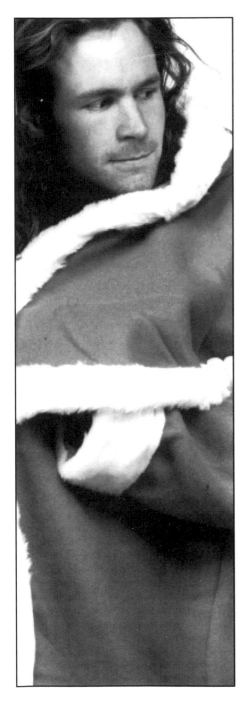

ing him off the edge of a fucking cliff. Dessie's adventures on the high moral ground were more illusory than real. But he made all the right noises, churning the stomachs of ordinary decent gombeens everywhere. For his frequent impersonations of a dog shitting razorblades, he has never fully gained the affections of the masses.

See Cox, Pat.

Ó'MAONLAÍ, Liam

The Hot House Flower was a gift to the Irish Language lobby, being hauled before the cameras at every possible opportunity to spout the *coopla fuckle*. Rock stars talk Irish too. Now this is progress. His inner journey has led him to bathe in the sea of a morning and to play the didgeridoo. His outer journey leads him to The Gig's Place for liver and chips after a skinful. He's a great bit of stuff.

Ó'MURCHÚ, Liam

With one foot in the present day, another foot in the Fifties, and both hands clinging on to the Middle Ages, he is the Bionic man of the Celtic experience. Throw in the fact that he can speak two languages simulteneously, and you are looking at a man apart. To illustrate his profound understanding of contemporary life, he uses the word "U2" in conversation. Duine uasal é, Billy Murphy.

Ó'MUIRCHEARTAIGH, Micheál

"And they're warming up the Christian Brother!" Micheál is rightly revered for such evocative ejaculations in the course of his thundering commentaries. The voice of Sunday afternoons, he gained immortality through an interview with Prince Edward after the Prince's greyhound had won a race at Wembley. And they're still warming up the Christian Brother.

O'REILLY, Tony

To give him his full title, as one must, Dr. A.J.F. O'Reilly is a man unlike other men. He is probably not even like Tony O'Reilly, such is the extravagance of his legend. Perhaps he is just a state of mind, an ethereal creation engineered in the Irish subconscious to satisfy our fantasies. I, for example, am not under the impression that I work for him, even though I do. I have backed his horses at Leopardstown, but I didn't see him there. Like God, you have to have faith in the existence of Tony O'Reilly.

O'RIORDAN, Dolores

If you ask about Dolores O'Riordan, the average punter will begin by talking about the wedding dress, and eventually make a passing comment about The Cranberries and their uplifting sound. This, and the odd ski-ing accident, is the price of success. You get to live in big houses, and to travel to exotic places, but you realise that everyone is talking about your underwear.

O'ROURKE, Colm

A Meath star for three generations, O'Rourke's survival is a triumph of optimism over experience. He never fails to show up on *The Sunday Game*, as billed, apparently sound in wind and limb, laughing and joking and wearing a nice jumper. One day Michael Lyster may have to announce that Colm couldn't make it tonight due to being held hostage and beaten savagely after a friendly Gaelic match. This is the way the game is going.

O'SÚILLEABHÁN, Micheál

A candidate in the Greatest Living Irishman stakes, he has rebelled against convention by attempting to popularise traditional Irish and classical music, where previous aficionadoes had done their damnedest to make them as unpopular as possible. He talks a great game

in a language that even total eejits can under-stand. Micheal The Evangelist.

O'SULLIVAN, Sonia

As her native Cobh threatens to sink into the sea, Sonya runs another blinder to cheer them up. Her defeat by the Chinese Daughters of Satan in the World Championships has forever darkened the Oriental peoples in the Irish mind. A caller to RTE criticised her for not hav-ing a proper Irish name, like Gobnait. A very good point there, sir. Did it take you long to think of that now?

O'TOOLE, Fintan

Being the only man in the world who under-stands the Beef Tribunal, Fintan became Heretic Number One in Fianna Fáil demonolo-gy. A Research Fellow in several Departments of the *Irish Times*, he is also the only man who has read Charles Haughey's *Spirit Of The Nation*, thus saving a lot of bother for every-one, including Charles Haughey. It is odds-on that he has read the Maastricht Treaty as well, and washed it down with a few ESRI Reports, thumbing through the 1983 Budget Speech for dessert. If anyone thinks they can pull a fast one by boring the arse off the punters, they have to get past Fintan O'Toole, the Man In The Gap.

PAISLEY, Ian

What's he doing here? Well, in Ireland, there's a welcome on the mat. For everyone. Whether they like it or not. Two images of Paisley: On BBC2's *Newsnight,* Jeremy Paxman intro-

duces an item on The North by telling us a story about a town in America which had a huge dunghill on the outskirts. Every day, a man would go out with his spade and dig away at the dunghill. His friends despaired of this, thinking it to be a total waste of time. But the man was steadfast. "With all of that horse-shit," he said, "there has to be a pony in there somewhere." Then Paxman turned to his hitherto unseen guest and said "Dr. Ian Paisley" . . . He did not get much further. A very ugly scene. On BBC1's *The Duty Men*, some customs officers were staking out a car in a Northern town, filming its owner selling bottles of poitín out of the boot. Paisley was simultaneously addressing a God-fearing gathering in the town square, and his voice could be heard hollering about the evils of the Devil's Buttermilk and John Barleycorn as the bottle of moonshine changed hands for a fiver. The moral? Much horse-shit, little pony.

PATTERSON, Frank

He has a lovely voice. A lovely, lovely, lovely voice. And so pleasant, so cheerful, with a little bit of a mischievous twinkle in the eye, and

lovely Eily tickling the ivories. Imagine himself and Finbarr Wright at it together, the Two Tenors, the Two Irish Tenors, with a satellite audience of four billion? Lovely, lovely, lovely.
See Wright, Finbarr.

PEARSON, Noel

The visionary impressario could look at Ireland's showband and cabaret stars and see them as ideal material for the roles of King Herod, Mary Magdalene, The Twelve Apostles, Jesus, Mary, and Holy Saint Joseph. He saw that Hollywood was waiting for the story of a disabled alcoholic from Crumlin, and for the grisly adventures of a mad Kerry farmer. He conquered Broadway with scenes of Donegal people dancing and telling lies. Others took LSD during the '60s. Pearson just looked into his heart and saw the big picture.
See Kenny, Tony.

PETERS, Red

It was not just his tremendous Blues voice that made him special, it was also the fact that he was a Customs inspector in Cavan or Monaghan or somewhere like that. That's The Blues for you. When the light catches it a certain way, his picture on a gig poster bears a passing resemblance to the bi-locationist, Padre Pio.
See Hanafin, Des.

PHELAN, Terry

The speedy full-back got a bit of a roasting from the loyalist hordes at Windsor Park for being both a Fenian and a person of colour.

He was a new species, a black Taig bastard. Given a more fortuitous roll of the dice, with Phelan, McGrath, Hughton, Babb and Fleming, we could have been on our way to an all-black Irish eleven. They're out there. Let's go for it.

POTTER, Maureen

The much-loved comedienne is a reminder of an era now vanished when people used to go to the Theatre to enjoy themselves. In the hey-day of Variety, there was no way that you would have to look at a couple of winos sitting in dustbins and howling at the moon. At least not on stage. Maureen is one of the few working actors who can remember performing in front of leading members of the German Nazi Party. Those lads don't go to the Theatre any more either.

PRATT, Maurice

The Face of Quinnsworth has found that the key to happiness lies in slashing prices and going on television to announce it, preferably in a funny hat. If only the likes of Sartre has known this, they might have made more of a fist of their existentialist deliberations. On television, Maurice has no discernible concept of embarrassment whatsoever.

See Dunne, Ben ; Quinn, Feargal ; Quinn, Pat.

PRENDERGAST, Peter

With no apparent discomfort, the brains behind Yoplait yogurt became the original National Handler, adding real fruit to Garret Fitzgerald's government. Did Garret need a handler? Well, consider this, from his *Irish Times* column: "And these multi-Party governments are going to have to address, hopefully in the wake of the re-establishment of peace and stability in Northern Ireland, quite new problems of fundamental importance to our society — most prominent among which will be that of securing a rational and socially just allocation of the very rapid increase in material resources per head of population that is starting to emerge as a consequence of a combination of faster economic growth with a rapid demographic decline in the previously very high ratio of dependents to workers." Indeed.
See FitzGerald, Garret.

PRONE, Terry

In bed at eight, up at four in the morning, she keeps similar hours to Con Houlihan, without the social life. The author of *"How To . . ."* books, she may wish to write one called *"How To Get Up Out Of Bed At 4 a.m."* As queen of Carr Communications, she helped Pee Flynn to be himself. Unfortunately, many of us wanted Pee to be someone else. She celebrated her book of short stories by appearing on the *Late Late Show* and announcing that she had lost five stones. The mystery was how she had put them on in the first place.
See Flynn, Padraig ; Houlihan, Con.

PURCELL, Deirdre

Actress, newsreader, journalist, and author of Gaybo's autobiography, her restless talent has found sanctuary in the strange world of the best-selling novel. Pseudish reviewers are unsure how to handle such material, as they fear that it is aimed at the hard-of-thinking, and that literature is diminished if it can be puchased along with Fig Rolls and packet soup. At least you can eat fig rolls after reading the blurb. Perhaps the greatest challenge for the best-selling novelist is that their novels have to be best-selling before anyone buys them.

PUSSY, Mister

Ireland's most revered drag queen now runs the hottest cafe in town, named after himself. He spotted a gap in the market for a place where you could consume a hearty Irish breakfast in the early hours, play bingo, and feast your eyes on an autographed copy of Naomi Campbell's knickers. How did we manage at all without it?

QUILL, Máirín

Before Máirín the Progressive Democrat bestrode the national stage, exuding common sense to no apparent purpose, the name Quill was renowned through the adventures of the bold Thaddeus, or "Thady" Quill, a Rabelaisian character by all accounts. *"For ramblin' for rovin' for football and courtin'/For drinkin' black porter as fast as they fill/In all your days rovin' you'll find none so jovial/as the Muskerry sportsman/The bould Thady Quill."* I wonder are they by any chance related?

QUINN, Fergal

The supermarket king and Senator is firmly on the side of what he chooses to call "the house-wife", making his Superquinn stores as user-friendly as can be, with plenty of fancy food thrown in to titillate the South Dublin palate. Fergal himself enjoys breakfast standing up, and insists on styling himself "a grocer", which is a bit like the Chief Executive of Shell describing himself as a petrol pump attendant. For recreation, he rides.

QUINN, Niall

Barring the odd Lucozade ad, Quinnie can't put a foot wrong. A gentleman and a scholar who can form sentences with a beginning, a middle and an end, he is the sort of person who makes political talent-scouts foam at the mouth, until they discover that he has a social conscience. Perhaps it was not a good idea for him to be wandering around Orlando as straight man to Brendan O'Carroll during the World Cup. But he will know not to do it again. See O'Carroll, Brendan.

QUINN, Pat

Remember him? Jesus, how could you ever

forget him? The spiritual progenitor of Maurice Pratt was the first man to identify himself with a supermarket chain, offering knock-down prices and the promise of a great time. The advertising suggested that if you were lucky, you would meet him at the checkout, wearing a funny hat and behaving flambuoyantly. A bit too flambuoyantly, perhaps. He is believed to be in Canada.

QUINN, Peter

Unusual for a man called Quinn, he never owned a supermarket chain, but he owned lots of other things which allowed him to devote his energies to the Presidency of the GAA. Here, he would address Congress on the evils of perfidious Dublin 4, the "liberal agenda", and other such excresences of West Britishness. Progressive as regards money, he floated the idea of Hurling as an Olympic sport. Ireland 6-37, Russia 0-3? We're onto a winner there.

QUINN, Ruairí

There was no smoked salmon left in Dublin Bay after Michael O'Leary quit the Labour Party, because Michael had eaten it all. Forced to survive on Michael's leftovers, Ruairí is doing his best in the circumstances. Ho Chi Quinn was once unbelievably left-wing, but he was young then, like Charlie Bird. He eventually found that life as a smooth operator was better craic, and the menus had a variety of smoked fish. In fairness, you never cringe when you see him meeting foreigners, and this is all we ask. He smoked marijuana as well, when he was young.

135

RABBITTE, Pat

The Democratic Left spokesperson on whatever you're having yourself takes his democracy seriously. Unlike some of his erstwhile colleagues in Stickie-land, he has no association with a time when men would change their name to Irish and go on "manouevres", seeking to unhinge the British Empire by pegging stones across the border. He looks like a normal person, and keeps up a steady stream of witticisms in the Dáil, hearing Minister Smith's voice on a crackly line from Medjugorje or dubbing Willie O'Dea "the Danny De Vito of Fianna Fáil." A great man for embarrassing the farmers.

REA, Stephen

He was nearly getting typecast as the most moody Northerner in showbiz, but is still capable of doing a turn in light comedy, or camping it up as Saint Oscar. Every article ever written about him refers to his marriage to Dolours Price, the famous bomber, and the fact that he doesn't talk about it. Then they try to get him to talk about not talking about it. God give him patience and another Neil Jordan project.

REID, Eileen

She has gone to God, her trying journey through the badlands of Cabaret ending in a reconciliation with her Maker. She sings and dances and appears on game shows in His name. She is Born Again, while some of her contemporaries ponder the wisdom of being born at all, only to die at the Braemor Rooms.

REYNOLDS, Albert

He owned a baker's dozen of ballrooms whose names ended in "land", as he plotted his rise to the summit of Ireland. At the Beef Tribunal, he gave a clue to his success by revealing that he took all of the best advice given to him and then ignored it. Originally a "Charlie Man", he is essentially an "Albert Man", and, of course, a one-sheet man. Addicted to foreign travel, he had a mission to "sell Ireland", but clearly never found a buyer. He looked set to become the first Taoiseach to land on the moon before the shit hit the fan big-time and he was forced to resign ignominiously. His followers still think that if he doesn't get a Nobel Prize for his

"peace process", he will almost certainly be made a saint. Curiously, Boris Yeltsin elected to get rat-arsed drunk rather than meet him at Shannon. Good call, Boris. A pioneer in terms of alcohol, his political philosophy may be described as teetotalitarianism.

RICE, Rodney

The gruff, genial, Northerner has spent a shocking amount of time in Leinster House, reporting the day's entertainment. Yet he remains gruff and genial, occasionally becoming genial and gruff, but always a Northerner. He gets out of the House by making frequent visits to the Third World. He thinks that you have to go abroad to find it.

ROACH, Hal

He has told jokes to five American Presidents. The Presidents come and go, the gags remain the same. The Waterford man is proud of the fact that he doesn't use "blue" material, and he feels pity for those that do, feeling particularly sorry for Eddie Murphy and Richard Pryor. The poor bastards. Though ensconced in Jury's Irish Cabaret for the last 1,400 years, he feels that a prophet is never recognised in his own land. Being a comedian and not a prophet, this doesn't apply to Hal.

ROBINSON, Mary

Red Robbo, too clever for her own good in the eyes of the backwoodsmen, transformed herself into the Queen of Ireland, inviting people to dance with her, and generally making the Presidency a full-time job. With husband Nick looming behind her, she eventually managed to eliminate a compulsive nodding movement from her repertoire of body language. In amassing scores of honorary degrees, she portrayed a glamorous, sophisticated image of Ireland which is sadly at variance with the truth. Fianna Fáil still prefer to think that it was all a freak accident, and that the Irish people wouldn't elect a liberal feminist to anything serious. She even goes to Gaelic matches now, something that she would not normally do. With our backsides to the wind, we salute her.

ROCCA, Michelle

She figured out that the only way to get a good interview out of Van Morrison was by becoming his muse. So now we know. What chance was there for Eamonn McCann?
See Morrison, Van.

ROCHA, John

One of those designer johnnies who are forever scoring triumphs for Irish fashion. In real life, he is a keen amateur footballer who plays in goal.

ROCHE, Stephen

During his *annus mirabilis*, Stephen wrested the Giro d'Italia away from team-mate Visentini, and then had the Tour De France wrested away from him by Charlie Haughey on the Champs Elysees. Words like "peleton" and "domestiques" entered the national vocabulary as the country went apeshit. Fearing Flann O'Brien's molecular theories, he retired before he became 75% bicycle. "How the hell did he do it?"

ROCK, Dickie

Before Punk Rock, there was Dickie Rock. "Spit on me, Dickie," they would ejaculate. A crooner in the classic mould, he survived the showband holocaust and is still with us. Miserly ballroom owners knew that he was a black belt in martial arts. In an unusually political move, he endorsed the candidature of John Stafford (FF) in the Euro elections. Stafford wanted us to vote for him because Dickie Rock said so. It was a tempting offer

which we refused in large numbers.
See Stafford, John.

ROGERS, John

In their long-running buddy movie, Dick Spring made his pardner Attorney-General while he was still a Junior Counsel. He certainly didn't make a balls of it like others we could mention, but won't, out of fear. When Dick is too busy to think, he turns to John, and John is always there for him.
See Spring, Dick.

ROGERS, Terry

He barked the odds and harangued the punters with great theatricality. When he stepped off his perch, the betting ring was a quieter place, and the mobile phone had usurped the ancient arts of the tic-tac man. You would feel bad about not giving Rogers your money. He felt that he deserved it.
See McManus, J.P.

ROLFE, Nigel

If it's Performance Art you're looking for, then Nigel is your only man. It is almost impossible to define Performance Art, but it can involve whipping out your cock on the *Late Late Show*, wearing a bucket over your head, or anything which challenges the status quo to recognise its inherent absurdity. Avoiding arrest can also be a problem. Nigel's favourite film is *Ju Dou*, a classic of the New Chinese cinema. My local video rental store doesn't seem to have an Old Chinese section, and has completely ignored the New Wave. ExtraVision, get the finger out!

ROSS, Shane

Scourge of the Unions, the Trinity Senator, stock-broker and journalist rails against the salaries of ICTU "barons", and decries their influence over the Government "partners". Though liberal on socio-sexual matters himself, he defended the right of the Catholic Church to issue its crazed submissions to the Cairo Conference on World Population. We know of people who "took the soup," and became Protestants. In his Cairo piece, Shane was looking like the first man to give back the soup. Recalling their wild years, his friend P.J. Mara described them as "things of beauty and boys forever." And in a way, you know, they still are.

See Attley, Bill; Mara, P.J.

ROSSA, Proinsias De

Along with Tomás Mac Giolla, he is one of the few living politicians who have been imprisoned for their beliefs, doing a bit of time in The

Curragh. He went in as Frank Ross and came out as Proinsias De Rossa, which has a better ring to it. They don't intern people for their political beliefs any more, but looking around the Dáil, it seems like an idea which has found its time again.

See Mac Giolla, Tomás; Rabbitte, Pat.

RYAN, Gerry

His training as a lawyer would have prepared him for the Sheep Tribunal, a heated inquisition into whether certain parties slaughtered a sheep in Connemara, or whether they were just pretending. Having passed this survival test, "Lambo" went on to pioneer Zoo radio on 2FM, and to host numerous TV programmes featuring ordinary people acting the bollocks. For recreation, he drinks whiskey and flies a helicopter, but not necessarily at the same time.

RYAN, Fr. Paddy

Few people had heard of the Pallottine Order before this turbulent priest achieved renown as a roving ambassador for the Republican movement, seeking out "the enemies of my enemy." During his Euro election campaign, he was accosted by television's Roger Cook, and challenged about his interpretation of the Commandment "thou shalt not kill". Ultimately he was done for robbing a caravan. A great man for going on hunger-strike.

See Malocca, Elio.

RYAN, Dr. Tony

GPA was a fabulous success story, with Tony

143

Ryan presiding over a team of free-booting executives whizzing around the globe cutting billion-dollar deals before breakfast, an example to us all. The likes of Garret Fitzgerald and Nigel Lawson were happy to be aboard this meteoric operation, and the man who gave us Ryanair was apparently on his way to making Howard Hughes look like a jumped-up baggage handler. He collected fine houses, fine paintings and fine pubs, and sponsored the Arts. Then it all went horribly, horribly, horribly, wrong. It was all you could do not to break your heart laughing.

RYNNE, Dr. Andrew

Doctor-with-attitude, his experiences at the Fleadh Ceoil with his friend Christy Moore gave him many insights into Irish ways and Irish laws, which he later put into practice by handing out rubber johnnies when it was neither profitable nor popular. The johnnies are everywhere now. For his pains, he was shot by a patient, inspiring the tabloid headline, "Sex Op Doc Shot". A good egg.

ST JOHN, Pete

Author of 'Dublin In The Rare Oul' Times' and 'The Fields Of Athenry', his cultural influence is incalculable, as are his royalties. His songs improve with drink.

SARGENT, Trevor

A Green, a Protestant, a clergyman, a TD, and a county councillor who objected to being bribed, he is a member of many minorities. In the Dáil, he played a recording of a hare being savaged by coursing dogs. A new and effective voice in the House.

SAVAGE, Tom

A force in Carr Communications, he treated Albert Reynolds for foot-in-mouth disease. He is married to Terry Prone, who gets up at four in the morning. Formerly a full-time priest, he would be used to the early starts.

SEX, Bill

The Kildare county footballer is an obvious target for jokes about dribbling before he shoots, or high, lobbing, dropping balls. Along with team-mate Anthony Rainbow, he makes Kildare the leading county for players with funny names.

SHANNON, Sharon

Billy Brown of The Freshman used to say that if there is music in Hell, it will be played on the accordion. Sharon makes the prospect of eternal damnation sound quite alluring.

SHATTER, Alan

On the liberal wing of Fine Gael, he appears to believe that it was reasonable to sit on the same benches as Oliver J. Flanagan, Alice Glenn, and Brendan McGahon, and still find personal fulfilment. Writing a steamy political novel may have eased his frustrations, but it buttered no parsnips when he heaved against John Bruton, and Bruton heaved back. Now he is on the condemned wing of Fine Gael.

SHEEHAN, John

The composer of 'The Marino Waltz' doesn't

drink. This is unusual among Irish fiddlers, but astonishing when you consider that he has toured the world with The Dubliners, who, shall we say, enjoyed a glass of wine with a meal. John preferred to come home to a nice turf fire.

See Drew, Ronnie; McKenna, Barney.

SHIELS, Brush

Teetotal, non-smoking, Brush's concept of the rock'n'roll lifestyle centres around sex and money and blathering all night long. Mr. Motormouth has challenged the urban/rural divide by settling in rural Meath, where he jousts with the natives in games of verbal agility amid the manure. His satin loon pants in mothballs, he now writes satirical verses about tractors.

SHERIDAN, Jim

"Shay" spent many years on the cutting edge of Theatre before the movies brought his exhilarating visions to the general public. It was a case of In The Name Of Jaysus as he spent many fruitless hours defending his Guildford Four film against accusations of artistic licence. He doesn't remember Dublin City in the rare oul' times, but he knows a lot of people who do.

SHINE, Brendan

When one thinks of Brendan, one immediately thinks of James Joyce. They say that if Dublin was ever destroyed in a freak accident, it could be reconstructed with the help of *Ulysses*. Similarly, if the Ordnance Survey records were ever wiped out, most of them could be replaced by consulting the works of Brendan Shine, and the wealth of geographical material contained therein. Like Joyce, Shine has a lovely, lovely, voice. If they are dissimilar in any way, it is that Shine has never written a masterpiece of 20th century literature.

SMITH, Michael

He mounted a complex defence of Albert Reynolds in the passports-for-dogfood scandal. His voice is so full of sincerity that it borders on the pious. He is such a good person that he finds it hard to see bad in anything. This is handy for a Minister for the Environment. He sounds more like a bishop than Michael Smith, the bishop.

SMURFIT, Michael

The Cardboard Box King is our man in Monte Carlo, where he is no doubt delighted to welcome The Irish who might stray there, wearing day-glo green hair, beating bodhrans, and standing under his window singing "Ole, Ole, Ole." A collector of horses and paintings, he has been known to bring his own wine to sip at functions. He is thinking of taking over China.

SMURFIT, Norma

A lady-who-lunches, whatever the hell that is, it was revealed that The General was thinking of kidnapping one of the Smurfit children, but cancelled the plan when he observed that Norma was a model mother, caring for her family just like a poor person. Michael backed another winner there.

147

SMYTH, Fr.Brendan

Like Fr. Paddy Ryan and the Pallottines, no-one had heard of the Norbertines until this man was imprisoned for a lifetime of child sex abuse, and being moved around by his superiors so that the Church wouldn't be embarrassed. Institutional abuse on this scale was not a revelation, more a confirmation in a rather public way of what sane people everywhere knew had been going on for years. It would be wrong to single him out just because he got caught. With any luck, the Church will have to pay zillions in compensation as thousands of actions are taken by the victims of its wicked, wicked ways. He brought down the Government.

See Casey, Bishop; Daly, Cardinal.

SMYTH, Sam G.

With his superb livery, Sam contradicts the general theory that the best journalists dress like Bowery bums. Equally proficient in the broadsheet and tabloid arts, his work has taken him to Bangkok, Las Vegas and Miami, where he endeared himself to the inhabitants with his easy charm and a range of cigarette tricks. "Life is too short for short stories."

SPRING, Dick

Like Ruairí Quinn, we do not cringe when we see Dick meeting foreigners, though on his visit to Bill Clinton after the Provo ceasefire, he bore a slight resemblance to a newly-released hostage. Ostensibly a man of the Left, neither Dick nor his father Dan were the sort of individuals who would curl up at night with the col-

148

lected works of V.I. Lenin. Thus he is able to tolerate co-habitation with a Fianna Fáil Party in which he once saw an "evil spirit" at work. He was the first Tánaiste to share his name with a sex toy.

See Rogers, John.

STAFFORD, John

His Euro election "literature" contained an endorsement from Dickie Rock, and photographs of the candidate with famous Irish footballers. "Vote for me because Dickie Rock likes me, and because I had my picture taken with Kevin Moran," was the message. He was also under the misapprehension that Jack Charlton endorsed his canditature, which made Jack rather angry. An apology ensued, though a life-sized model of Mr. Stafford was found hanging from a tree in Fairview Park, bearing the message, "Apology Not Accepted – Jack". He got slaughtered.

STAPLETON, Frank

In the bad old days, when Stapo scored for Ireland, a nation would look to the linesman, the referee, and sometimes into the abyss, as the bastards disallowed the goal for no good reason. Now that we are aristocrats of the world game, we can celebrate in comfort. They say that Stapo was possibly the best, but definitely the best-paid striker in England.

STAUNTON, Stephen

"Stan" reversed the practice of generations by putting on his hat for the National Anthem in the terrible heat of Orlando. There are times when he looks more like a Gaelic player, and his knack of scoring direct from corner-kicks is reminiscent of the "line ball". When he keeps it under the bar, he is invaluable.

STEMBRIDGE, Gerry

Instrumental in *Scrap Saturday*, the Limerick man has experimented with forms of Theatre which might be relevant to the general public. In a TV drama, he created a Pro-Life character who drinks his own piss. Gerry doesn't drink either alcohol or piss, but still contributes much to the gaiety of the nation.

STEPHENSON, John

Forever young, he orchestrated the "Flaming Door" festival commemorating 1916, causing revisionists to cry "Flaming Nora!". Now he looks forward to orchestrating the Millenium shenanigans. In life, he has favoured the grand gesture, holding a Crucifixion Party to celebrate his 33rd birthday. Doubtless it was his tendency towards republican and messianic imagery which had him being mooted as a possible Fianna Fáil candidate. The mind boggles.

STEPHENSON, Sam

One never fails to admire his controversial Civic Offices, their clean, uncluttered facade standing in bold contrast to the fussy medievalism of Christchurch. His Central Bank is a brash homage to Mammon which dwarfs the pretentious cobblestones and sinister alleyways of Temple Bar in every respect. And what does he get? Dog's abuse.

151

STOKES, Niall

Long-haired editor of *Hot Press* and chairperson of the IRTC, Niall takes a trenchant editorial line on all issues, particularly socio-religious ones, where his frequent calls for the resignation of the Pope have caused much unease in Church circles, and indeed in the Vatican itself. He has let it be known in no uncertain terms that he is in favour of sexual intercourse, fellatio, cunnilingus, and a whole range of entertainments besides, but that he is totally opposed to plane crashes.

STEWART-LIBERTY, Nell

A quare name but great stuff.
See Burke-Kennedy, Mary Elizabeth; Frisbee, Mai.

STUART, Francis

Don't mention the War! Stuart has never quite lived down his unfortunate associations with Nazi Germany, an association which perversely suits his conception of the artist as an outcast from society. His remarkable physical appearance is redolent of the etchings of children, accentuating his sense of being different from the herd. He's a divil for the nags.

STUART, Gene

The Mighty Avons frontman never trod the lonely artistic road of his namesake, Francis, but he has no unfortunate associations with Nazi Germany.

SUTHERLAND, Peter

The ample-bottomed "Bunter" has fired all of our imaginations as he leaps from one big job to another. It is as though our well-being as a nation is directly linked to the magnitude of "Bunter's" next meal ticket. He would have become President of the European Commission if he had been asked nicely, and if Pee Flynn's bottom hadn't been in the way. Quality-of-life is what matters to him now.
See Fitzgerald, Dr.Garret; Flynn, Padraig.

TAYLOR, Mervyn

The Minister for Equality and Law Reform is perhaps best known for his distinctive grey slip-on shoes. It has fallen to him to pave the way for Divorce. The lucky so-and-so.

TOIBIN, Niall

So evocative are his renditions of regional accents that people who attempt the Cork or Cavan patois are actually impersonating Niall Toibin's impersonation. An exceptionally funny person with a hint of menace, he is very good at playing mad bastards. Reputed to be "irascible" in interviews, I found him to be the heart and soul of cordiality. So "iracible" is wrong. It should be "cordial".

TOM, Big

It came as some surprise to his millions of fans when Big Tom was accused by a one-time female lover of waging a campaign of harrassment which involved him playing his recordings over the phone to her at unsocial hours, leaving a copy of his latest video, audio cassette and CD in her home, and eating the contents of her fridge. A gaggle of girls had once completely ignored Mick Jagger in order to get Tom's autograph. Jagger asked to be introduced, and Tom said, "you look just like him too." His innocence was further demonstrated by the fact that his band was called the Mainliners, a slang term for intravenous heroin users. Innocent until proven guilty, sez you. How Big can you get?

TOWNSEND, Andy

The first captain of the Republic to dye for the cause, he has otherwise avoided social embarrasment with his ready wit and charm.

During his Chelsea days, thugs were heard to roar in broad Cockney, "Townsend, you Oirish bastard!" Finally, he was one of us.

TREACY, John

The long-distance runner par excellence, he conquered the mucky world of Cross Country, and struck silver in the Marathon in the terrible heat of Los Angeles. No doubt he was very chuffed to be hailed on his arrival in Dublin by Senator Donie Cassidy. "He seems so frail."

TREACY, Olivia

Miss Ireland became Lady Chatterley, the first holder of the crown to play a serious theatrical role since Yvonne Costello. Her career has developed to encompass light journalism. So beautiful, so talented.
See Costello, Yvonne.

TREACY, Sean

The Ceann Comhairle, with his splendid robes and his hammer poised, moderates the proceedings of the House with much gravitas. Not only does he have to listen to this shit, he has to stop any mischief before it starts, thus minimising the possibility of craic. As they leave, they bow to him. It is all very sad.

TURKEY, Dustin The

Many have remarked on the strange fact that a stuffed toy is easily the best thing on RTE. During the Presidential election, the likeable Dubliner is said to have outpolled Austin Currie in certain constituencies. He has campaigned to bring the DART to Dingle and reached No.1

in the Irish charts. For a turkey this was not unusual. But he rose above it all.

WALSH, Ted

The man who introduced "super leppers" and "leery oul' buggers" to RTE's racing team has offered some typically canny advice on the subject of the Galway Races. If you're thinking of going there, you should take out a five-pound note, and throw it in the fire. Watch it burn, and if you can stand the pain, then go to Galway.

WARNER, Dick

During his ravishing *Waterways* series, Warner had a flashback to his days in Haight-Ashbury, and rode a big motorbike around Portumna. This delightful touch was criticised by viewers of Arthur Murphy's *Mailbag,* who pointed out that he was not wearing a helmet. Clever, clever.
See Murphy, Arthur.

WATKINS, Kathleen

Her Ireland is full of nice people doing interesting things in glorious weather — an Ireland which for better or for worse remains hidden to most of us. Every day she lives out the fantasy of thousands of women by receiving a private audience with Gay Byrne. But they don't hate her for it if it makes him happy.

WHELEHAN, Harry

The least likely newspaper headline used to be "Farmers Are Happy". In the time of Harry Whelehan, it was overtaken by "Attorney-

General: No Controversy Today". Apart from scheming barristers, no-one gave a shit about the Attorney-General before this extraordinary man came along. Well, there was the Attorney-General in whose apartment Malcolm McArthur rested up after his stint in the killing fields. That was controversial. That was a hard act to follow. But cometh the hour cometh the man. "Albert" gave him the job he had promised him, as President of the High Court and then it all went horribly, horribly, horribly wrong. Currently practicing as a barrister. Or not as the case may be. "I am President of the High Court." Not any more your're not.

See MacArthur, Malcolm.

WILKINSON, Colm

"The Blade", as he was known in the lounges, made a line about "walking down Grafton Street to Neary's Bar, for a jar" sound cathartic. Never had the lunchtime scoop been rendered with such raw passion. A man of such operatic leanings was bound to find himself in musicals, where he achieved world domination through *Les Miserables*, playing the part of the hero, Les.

WILSON, John

Another illustrious product of the Cavan Gaelic Football system, he served in many governments without quite reaching the top of the slippery pole. This may be attributed to his penchant for speaking in Greek and Latin at every available opportunity. He brought a little bit of Rome to Ballyjamesduff.

WOGAN, Terry

The thinking man's Henry Kelly, Wogan is a spiritual kinsman to Brian Lenihan, appearing less intelligent than he actually is. He refuses to rise above the triviality of it all, sensing the brevity of life. For some reason, he is better at acting the bollocks on radio than on television. Thus, Eurovision is his ideal medium, a radio commentary for television on people acting the bollocks. He has opened many doors for the Irish, usually at supermarkets.

WRIGHT, Finbarr

He has a lovely, lovely, lovely, voice. It is as though Frank Patterson has handed on the torch, keeping alive the tradition of the Irish Tenor. But hey, Frank's not finished either! Frank can still give it a bit of welly. If anything, Finbarr has a superior pedigree, having studied for the priesthood. Frank only looks like a man of the cloth, betrayed by that twinkle in the eye. Lovely, lovely, lovely.
See Patterson, Frank.

ZAG, Zig And

A brilliant creation, they became so entrenched in the national consciousness that politicians trying to be funny would inevitably reach for that "Zig And Zag" analogy, expecting total hilarity to ensue. Then they fled to Channel 4, leaving a generation of Irish children to mourn. Fuck them.